高职

U0682109

A Training Course for English Tour Guides

涉外导游技能实训

鲍旦旦　孙建中　主　编

支静文　崔　竞　屠玉蓉　舒　江　潘　玥　副主编

江苏大学出版社
JIANGSU UNIVERSITY PRESS

镇　江

图书在版编目(CIP)数据

涉外导游技能实训/鲍旦旦,孙建中主编. —镇江:
江苏大学出版社,2016.8
ISBN 978-7-5684-0303-0

Ⅰ.①涉… Ⅱ.①鲍… ②孙… Ⅲ.①导游-英语-
教材 Ⅳ.①F590.633

中国版本图书馆 CIP 数据核字(2016)第 216237 号

涉外导游技能实训

Shewai Daoyou Jineng Shixun

主　　编/鲍旦旦　孙建中
副 主 编/支静文　崔　竞　屠玉蓉　舒　江　潘　玥
责任编辑/韦雅琪　米小鸽
出版发行/江苏大学出版社
地　　址/江苏省镇江市梦溪园巷 30 号(邮编:212003)
电　　话/0511-84446464(传真)
网　　址/http://press.ujs.edu.cn
排　　版/镇江文苑制版印刷有限责任公司
印　　刷/虎彩印艺股份有限公司
开　　本/718 mm×1 000 mm　1/16
印　　张/12.75
字　　数/320 千字
版　　次/2016 年 8 月第 1 版　2016 年 8 月第 1 次印刷
书　　号/ISBN 978-7-5684-0303-0
定　　价/32.00 元

如有印装质量问题请与本社营销部联系(电话:0511-84440882)

前　言

Preface

高职院校的涉外导游技能实训课程是一门跨学科、综合性、实践性、技能性的课程。与传统课程相比,涉外导游技能实训课程在开设的时间和空间上需作延伸和拓展;课程教学要以实践为主线,以技能为主题,以应用为目的;课程的考核不能局限于第一课堂,应贯穿于学生的学习、实训、实习等全过程,要不拘一格、全方位进行考察,以学生涉外导游服务职业技能的实质性习得与提高为目标和评价依据。

在深入走访行业及专家的基础上,我们以完成一条目前入境游的经典线路的接待服务为目的,紧紧围绕准备工作、接团服务、商讨行程、住宿餐饮、游览服务、购物服务、送团服务、特殊问题处理等典型工作场景,按照这些工作任务的要求来编写教材,内容环环相扣、实用有效、可操作性强。每一个训练项目由任务引入开始,以实训任务为载体组织项目实施,突出任务所需的具体操作步骤、知识和技能,同时辅以必要的范例、对话、语言点归纳、实用小贴士和相关知识链接等,引导学生按照工作步骤完成系列实训任务,并实现课程学习自我评价和教师评价的结合。

本教材具有以下特点:

第一,以职业活动为背景设计工作场景。借鉴和使用涉外导游岗位标准和相关企业内训资料,结合现代涉外旅游企业文化建设要求,精心设计模拟场景,加深学生对涉外导游知识与职业技能的领悟,准确掌握行业规范,熟练运用语言和导游服务技能。

第二,以任务为驱动,以项目为导向设计实训内容。以涉外导游服务工作流程为主线,以涉外导游的真实工作内容为学习任务,围绕准备工作、接团服务、商讨行程、住宿餐饮、游览服务、购物服务、送团服务、特殊问题处理等任务来设计教材内容。

第三,构建知识学习与技能训练高度融合的"工学结合"教材体例。以模块为纲领,把每个具体模块分解为若干工作任务,按照任务的提出、任务的实施、任务的完成、任务的评价的思路设计实训步骤和方法。从职业角度着手,以知识与实践并重、教学与训练结合为原则，以涉外导游知识和英语语言技能实用、适用、够用为准则，强化学生职业能力培养，同时注重学生的个性发展。

第四，分层次、有步骤地设计实训任务，体现科学性和可操作性。课内、课外相结合，校内、校外相补充。既有以学生反复练习和体验训练为主的单项技能的强化训练，又有模拟工作过程的综合性训练，体现"做中学""学中做"的学练原则。

在本教材的编写过程中，我们参阅了不少方家大作，并参考、摘引了有关报刊、专著和网络资料，特此说明，一并对相关作者表示衷心的感谢。与此同时，我们也要感谢镇江市高等专科学校和江苏大学出版社对本书出版给予的大力支持，感谢出版社编辑同志付出的辛劳。

由于时间仓促，加之水平有限，本教材尚存在一些不足之处，恳请各位读者、同行和专家批评指正，并及时反馈给我们，以便我们在教学实践中改正或再版时修订。

编　者

2016 年 7 月

目 录

Contents

导 入

Introduction

　　根据涉外导游接待服务规范,地接社导游要认真阅读、研究、熟悉接团计划,做好充分的接待准备,提供接团、住宿、餐饮、景点游览、购物、送团等优质服务,圆满完成导游服务工作。本教程以接待一个来自澳大利亚的访华旅游团为工作场景,让学习者在8个设定的实训模块中进行系统的学习训练,把他们培养成合格的涉外导游。

　　In accordance with the English tour guide service specifications, tour guides from local travel agencies are required to read, study and get familiar with the tour plan, make good preparations, provide high-quality service in such processes as meeting on arrival, accommodation, catering, scenic spot sightseeing, shopping, seeing off and so on, and thus successfully complete the guiding work. This training course reproduces the typical work settings of the local tour guides giving service to a tour group from Australia visiting China in the form of 8 modules. In the modules, students receive a systematic training and do plenty of practice to achieve the aim to work as qualified English tour guides.

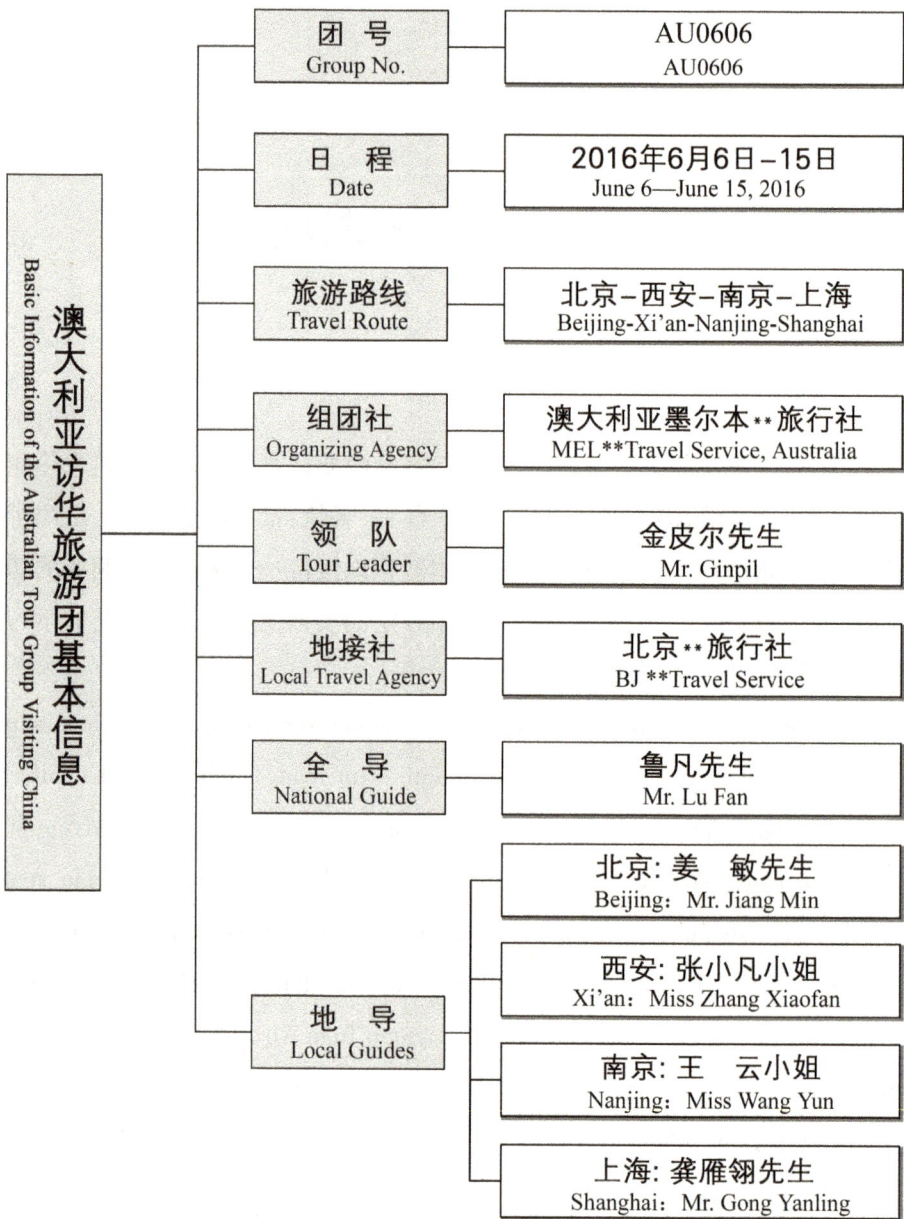

澳大利亚访华旅游团基本信息 Basic Information of the Australian Tour Group Visiting China	团　号 Group No.	AU0606 AU0606
	日　程 Date	2016年6月6日-15日 June 6—June 15, 2016
	旅游路线 Travel Route	北京-西安-南京-上海 Beijing-Xi'an-Nanjing-Shanghai
	组团社 Organizing Agency	澳大利亚墨尔本**旅行社 MEL**Travel Service, Australia
	领　队 Tour Leader	金皮尔先生 Mr. Ginpil
	地接社 Local Travel Agency	北京**旅行社 BJ **Travel Service
	全　导 National Guide	鲁凡先生 Mr. Lu Fan
	地　导 Local Guides	北京：姜　敏先生 Beijing：Mr. Jiang Min
		西安：张小凡小姐 Xi'an：Miss Zhang Xiaofan
		南京：王　云小姐 Nanjing：Miss Wang Yun
		上海：龚雁翎先生 Shanghai：Mr. Gong Yanling

模块一 准备工作

Module 1 Making Preparations

任务描述 Task Description

准备工作是导游工作的开端,是导游工作程序中重要的一环,为后续工作打下良好的基础。导游在接受任务后,要做好准备工作,按时前往指定地点迎接旅游团。准备工作主要包括熟悉接待计划和落实接待事宜。

Making preparations is the beginning of the guide work, and as an important part in the whole business, it helps to lay a good foundation for the follow-up work. After being given the task, the tour guide must get ready to meet the tourists at the appointed place on time. Making preparations includes studying the reception plan and getting everything ready.

任务目标 Learning Objectives

1. 熟悉接待计划。

Get familiar with the reception plan.

2. 能够使用英语处理文书工作和进行口语交流,掌握相关的基本词汇和表达。

Be able to use English freely in paper work and communication. Master the basic words and expressions concerned.

3. 培养计划意识,养成按计划办事的习惯。

Develop planning consciousness and the habit of being well-organized at work.

工作流程 Working Process

1. 了解旅游团的相关信息。阅读接待计划和有关资料,详细了解该旅游团的服务项目和要求等信息,主要包括以下几个方面:

Read the reception plan and the related materials carefully and get relevant information about the service items and demands as listed below.

(1) 签发单位(即组团社),联络人的姓名及电话号码,领队、全程导游、地接导游的姓名及联系电话。

travel agency that organizes the tour group, name(s) of the contact person(s) and their telephone number(s), names and telephone numbers of the tour leader, the national guide and the local guide(s)

(2) 旅游团的名称、代号、电脑序号、国别、语言、收费标准(豪华、标准、经济)、结算方式。

name, code, computer serial number, origin country, language, fee scale (luxury, standard, economy) and way of payment of the tour group

(3) 旅游团的基本情况:人数、姓名、性别、职业、宗教信仰等。

group's information: total number, names, genders, occupations, religions and so on

(4) 出入境地点、全程旅游路线、行程等信息。

group's exit-entry ports, tour route and itinerary

(5) 食宿安排情况及特殊服务要求。

hotel accommodation, restaurant arrangements and requirements for special service

(6) 所乘交通工具情况:机场(火车站、码头)的名称、航班号、到达及出发时间等。

arrival and departure transport information: names of airports (railway stations, ports), flight numbers and times

(7) 交通票据情况:预订、有无变更。

transport tickets: reservations, ticket change

2. 落实接待事宜。主要包括交通车辆、住宿和用餐安排、景点开放情况等内容。

Confirm the items such as transport vehicles, accommodation and meals, opening hours of the scenic spots and so on.

（1）与全程导游联系，约定接团的时间和地点；备齐有关旅行社、餐厅、酒店、司机及其他相关人员的联系方式等信息。

Contact the national guide, fix the time and place to meet the group; get the telephone numbers of the travel agency, restaurants, hotels, drivers and other relevant persons.

（2）与提供交通服务的车队或汽车公司联系，问清、核实司机的姓名、车号、联系电话。

Contact the transport service or company and obtain or confirm the driver's name, the bus number, and the contact telephone number.

（3）接大型旅游团时，车上应贴编号或醒目的标记。

For a large tour group, make sure the bus is labeled with numbers or attractive marks.

（4）确定与司机的接头地点并告知活动的日程和具体时间。

Make clear the location where you will meet the driver, and inform the driver of the schedule and the exact time.

（5）落实房间及用餐预订，核实房间数、级别、是否含早餐，告知抵店时间。

Confirm the hotel and restaurant reservations. Check the number and the standard of the rooms, and whether breakfast is included in the room rate. Notify the hotel of the arrival time of the group.

（6）熟悉旅游团所住酒店的名称、位置、概况、服务设施和服务项目。

Be familiar with the hotel's name, location, general profile, service facilities and service items.

（7）与有关餐厅联系，确认该团日程表上安排的每一次用餐的情况，其中包括日期、团号、用餐时间、用餐人数、餐饮标准、特殊要求（饮食禁忌）等。

Contact the restaurants in advance to confirm each meal on the schedule, including the date, group number, meal time, number of tourists, catering standard and special requirements(food taboos), etc.

（8）落实行李运送服务。

Arrange baggage delivery service.

（9）了解景点的情况，对新的旅游景点或不熟悉的参观游览点，要充分了解和研究其情况,搞清开放时间、最佳游览路线、洗手间位置等,以便游览活动顺利进行。

Get enough information about the scenic spots. For those new or unfamiliar scenic spots, make a careful study of them in advance. Be clear about their opening time, the best tour route, restroom locations, etc. to make everything go smoothly.

(10) 准备以下物品和信息:

Get the following things ready for use or reference.

① 详细的旅游行程

detailed itinerary

② 乘客名单、分房名单

passenger name list and rooming list

③ 预约信息(有联系方名称):包括地面运营商、酒店、交通等

booking information (with names of the contact parties) including ground operators, hotels, transportation, etc.

④ 交通票据,包括机票、火车票等

transport tickets including air tickets, train tickets, etc.

⑤ 所有费用的财务结算表

accounting sheets for all expenses

⑥ 支票或付款凭证

checks or vouchers for payments

⑦ 行李标签(牌)

luggage tags

⑧ 特殊事件处理预案

special problem and emergency handling plan

⑨ 旅行社旗

flag of the travel agency

⑩ 姓名徽章

name badges

小贴士Tips

旅游团团号

旅游团团号编码可以由组团社名称大写拼音或英文首字母和相应的出发日期组成,例如,南京龙源国际旅行社 2015 年 6 月 6 日发团的旅游团的团号就可编为 NJLY150606。

独立成团

独立成团是指旅游者不论人数多少,单独包车、聘请导游提供专属服务的旅游团队,一般由单位、公司、家庭或朋友组成。这样的团队人数比较多,独立成团的成员几乎都认识。独立成团使旅游者更好地享受旅游、品味旅游,是一种个性化的时尚旅游方式。旅游者自行选择旅游景点、设计旅游线路,有更充裕的游览参观时间,具有很高的自由度。由于其产品具有针对性,服务具有专一性,因此其品质和服务质量远高于常规旅游方式。不过独立成团需要提前预订和安排,旅游价格相对较高。

散客拼团

散客拼团是一种常规的、经济的、大众化的旅行方式。它由来自不同地方的散客或在各旅行社营销点分散报名的游客组团。旅行社因受旅行车座位和经营成本的限制,根据不同的路线,定有不同的最低成团人数。如果人数不足,可以由在其他旅行社报名的旅客补充组团。散客团成员通常互相不认识,旅行社决定旅游景点、旅游线路和游览参观时间,游客自由度较低。

课堂实训　In-class Practice

实训项目 1　Task 1

实用写作：熟悉接待计划

Practical Writing：Study the Reception Plan

实训要求：现有来自澳大利亚的 18 人旅游团,你是他们在北京期间的导游,旅行社提供了接待计划(表 1-1、表 1-2),要求认真准备,做好服务。阅读接待计划书,准确掌握接待内容和要求,完成工作备忘录的填写任务。

Directions: Here is a tour group of 18 people from Australia. You will be the local guide during their stay in Beijing. The travel agency gives a reception plan to you (Form 1-1, Form 1-2), and demands your good preparation for serving the group. Study the given reception plan, understand and grasp the task requirements, and fill in the working memo followed.

表1-1 北京 ∗∗ 旅行社接待计划
Form 1-1   Reception Plan of __BJ ∗∗__ Travel Agency

<u>姜敏先生</u>:根据工作安排,你将负责接待一个澳大利亚旅游团,他们将于<u>6月6日</u>抵达<u>北京</u>,请做好接待准备。

Tour guide __Mr. Jiang Min__: According to the working arrangements, you are going to serve an Australian tour group which will arrive at __Beijing__ on __June 6__. Please get prepared.

旅游路线 Travel Route	北京—西安—南京—上海 Beijing-Xi'an-Nanjing-Shanghai		日程 Date	2016 年 6 月 6 日—15 日 June 6—June 15, 2016	
团号 Group No.	AU0606	国籍 Nationality (Region)	澳大利亚 Australia	Number of Persons 游客人数	18 人:男性 10, 女性 8(儿童 2) 18: male 10, female 8(child 2)
订餐标准 Meals	早:自助餐 20 元/人 中:桌餐 30 元/人 晚:桌餐 50 元/人 (均不含酒水)	Breakfast: buffet 20 RMB/person Lunch: table meal 30 RMB/person Supper: table meal 50 RMB/person (Wine and beverage are not included in the price.)			
订房标准 Room	四星级酒店 Four-star hotels				
往返航班时间 **Flight Schedule (entry and exit)**	到达:6 月 6 日 CA1∗∗ 航班 9:15 到达北京首都国际机场 Arrival: 9:15 on June 6, CA1∗∗, Beijing Capital International Airport (PEK)				
	离开:6 月 15 日 CA1∗∗ 航班 21:30 离开上海浦东国际机场(组团社代订) Departure: 21:30 on June 15, CA1∗∗, Shanghai Pudong International Airport (PVG) (Booked by organizing agency)				

续表

组团社 Organizing Agency	澳大利亚墨尔本 ** 旅行社 MEL ** Travel Service, Australia	联系人 Contact Person	艾伦女士 Ms. Alan	联系电话 Contact Number	0061 89 ** 444269
地接社 Local Travel Agency	北京 ** 旅行社 BJ ** Travel Service	联系人 Contact Person	童阳先生 Mr. Tong Yang	联系电话 Contact Number	010-53 ** 0062 158 ** 039599
全导 National Guide	鲁凡先生 Mr. Lu Fan	联系电话 Contact Number	133 ** 647643	领队 Tour Leader	金皮尔先生 Mr. Ginpil 139 ** 743300
结算形式 Way of Payment	包游(吃饭、住宿、 交通、游园票) Package Tour (including meals, rooms, transport, entrance tickets)	服务等级 Grade	特优级 Wonder Service	特殊服务 Special Service	老人:3 人 3 seniors 素食者:5 人 5 vegetarians 儿童:2 人 2 children
接待信息 Contact Information	北京:北京 ** 旅行社 Beijing:BJ ** Travel Service	童先生 Mr. Tong, 158 ** 039599			
		地导:姜敏先生 Local guide:Mr. Jiang Min, 136 ** 321369			
	西安:西安 ** 旅行社 Xi'an:XA ** Travel Service	张女士 Ms. Zhang, 139 ** 582631			
		地导:张小凡小姐 Local guide:Miss Zhang Xiaofan, 189 ** 764500			
	南京:南京 ** 旅行社 Nanjing:NJ ** Travel Service	李先生 Mr. Li, 138 ** 806513			
		地导:王云小姐 Local guide:Miss Wang Yun, 150 ** 442435			
	上海:上海 ** 旅行社 Shanghai:SH ** Travel Service	罗女士 Ms. Luo, 139 ** 256189			
		地导:龚雁翎先生 Local guide:Mr. Gong Yanling, 130 ** 889322			

续表

		Itinerary			
城市 City	到达/离开时间 Arrival/ Departure Time	住宿酒店 Hotel Arrangement	餐饮安排 Meal Arrangement	行程 Travel Activities	备注 Note
北京 Beijing	航班CA1** 于6月6日9:15到达北京;航班 CA3*** 于6月10日9:25赴西安 Flight CA1** arrives at 9:15 on June 6, Flight CA3*** to Xi'an at 9:25 on June 10	北京香格里拉饭店 Beijing Shangri-la Hotel	早4+中4+晚4 4B+4L+4D 1次豪华午餐:北京烤鸭晚餐 A Special Royal lunch: Beijing Duck Dinner	天安门广场、故宫、熊猫馆、颐和园、长城、十三陵、天坛、观看京剧 Tian'anmen Square, Forbidden City, Panda Hall, Summer Palace, Great Wall, Ming Tombs, Temple of Heaven, Watch Beijing Opera	北京首都国际机场 Beijing Capital International Airport (PEK)
西安 Xi'an	航班CA3*** 于6月10日11:20到达西安;航班MU8*** 于6月11日16:10赴南京 Flight CA3*** arrives at 11:20 on June 10, Flight MU8*** to Nanjing at 16:10 on June 11	西安赛瑞喜来登酒店 Sheraton Xi'an North City Hotel	早1+中2+晚1 1B+2L+1D 1次当地特色餐:羊肉泡馍 A Local Speciality: Pita Bread Soaked in Lamb Soup	秦始皇兵马俑博物馆、古城墙、大雁塔、回民街 Museum of Qin Shi Huang Terracotta Warriors and Horses, City Wall, Big Wild Goose Pagoda, Muslim Quarter	西安咸阳国际机场 Xi'an Xianyang International Airport (XIY)
南京 Nanjing	航班MU8*** 于6月11日18:35到达南京;高铁G75** 于6月14日7:20前往上海 Flight MU8*** arrives at 18:35 on June 11, G75** by CRH (China Railway Highspeed) to Shanghai at 7:20, on June 14	南京金陵饭店 Nanjing Jinling Hotel	早3+中2+晚3 3B+2L+3D (地方特色菜 Local Dishes)	中山陵、明孝陵、灵谷寺、红山森林动物园、长江大桥、总统府、秦淮风光带、夫子庙 Dr. Sun Yat-sen's Mausoleum, Ming Tomb, Linggu Temple, Hongshan Forest Zoo, Yangtze River Bridge, Presidential Palace, Qinhuai Scenic Zone, Confucius Temple	南京禄口国际机场 Nanjing Lukou International Airport (NKG)

续表

Itinerary					
城市 City	到达/离开时间 Arrival/ Departure Time	住宿酒店 Hotel Arrangement	餐饮安排 Meal Arrangement	行程 Travel Activities	备注 Note
上海 Shanghai	高铁G75 ∗∗ 于6月14日8:45到达上海;航班CA1 ∗∗ 于6月15日晚21:30返程 G75 ∗∗ arrives at 8:45 on June 14 Flight CA1 ∗∗ departs at 21:30 on June 15.	上海世纪皇冠假日酒店 Shanghai Crowne Plaza Century Park	早1+中2+晚2 1B+2L+2D (地方特色菜 Local Dishes)	购物游 Shopping 上海博物馆、东方明珠广播电视塔、老城区购物市场、上海金融中心、正大广场 Shanghai Museum, Oriental Pearl Radio & TV Tower, Old Town Market, Shanghai Financial Center, Super Brand Mall	上海浦东国际机场 Shanghai Pudong International Airport (PVG)
备注 Note	北京随团司机 Beijing bus driver	张福先生 Mr. Zhang Fu(京B33 ∗∗∗ ,139 ∗∗ 473210)			
	西安随团司机 Xi'an bus driver	刘云先生 Mr. Liu Yun(陕A28 ∗∗∗ ,138 ∗∗ 589123)			
	南京随团司机 Nanjing bus driver	马乐先生 Mr. Ma Le(苏A90 ∗∗∗ ,138 ∗∗ 463782)			
	上海随团司机 Shanghai bus driver	胡良先生 Mr. Hu Liang (沪D61 ∗∗∗ ,138 ∗∗ 879041)			

表 1-2　游客名单(16 成人,2 儿童)

Form 1-2　Tourist Information (16 adults, 2 children)

序号 Serial Number	姓名 Name	年龄 Age	性别 Sex	国籍 Nationality	职业 Occupation	备注 Note
1	Amarijit Cooper	46 岁(丈夫) 46(husband)	男 male	澳大利亚 Australia	律师 lawyer	肥胖 obesity 素食者 vegetarian
2	Ella Cooper	37 岁(妻子) 37(wife)	女 female	澳大利亚 Australia	教师 teacher	糖尿病 diabetes 素食者 vegetarian

续表

序号 Serial Number	姓名 Name	年龄 Age	性别 Sex	国籍 Nationality	职业 Occupation	备注 Note
3	Miller Cooper	5 岁（女儿） 5（daughter）	女 female	澳大利亚 Australia		
4	Davis Cooper	6 岁（儿子） 6（son）	男 male	澳大利亚 Australia		
5	Annelie Wilson	22 岁 22	女 female	澳大利亚 Australia	大学生 undergraduate	
6	Heldoorm Carter	42 岁（丈夫） 42（husband）	男 male	澳大利亚 Australia	销售经理 sales manager	支气管炎 bronchitis
7	Wayne Carter	40 岁（妻子） 40（wife）	女 female	澳大利亚 Australia	设计师 designer	素食者 vegetarian
8	Kewell Walker	31 岁 31	女 female	澳大利亚 Australia	会计 accountant	
9	Siew Lewis	50 岁 50	女 female	澳大利亚 Australia	咨询师 consultant	酒精过敏 allergic to alcohol
10	Jerryoo Thong	58 岁 58	男 male	澳大利亚 Australia	教师 teacher	
11	Jone Hudson	68 岁（丈夫） 68（husband）	男 male	澳大利亚 Australia	商人 merchant	
12	Emily Hudson	67 岁（妻子） 67（wife）	女 female	澳大利亚 Australia	教师 teacher	素食者 vegetarian
13	Chloe Noah	21 岁 21	male 男	澳大利亚 Australia	大学生 undergraduate	
14	Jack Green	38 岁（丈夫） 38（husband）	male 男	澳大利亚 Australia	教师 teacher	
15	Aria Green	36 岁（妻子） 36（wife）	female 女	澳大利亚 Australia	销售经理 sales manager	素食者 vegetarian
16	Lily Baker	43 岁 43	male 男	澳大利亚 Australia	会计 accountant	甲状腺亢进 hyperpara- thyroidism

续表

序号 Serial Number	姓名 Name	年龄 Age	性别 Sex	国籍 Nationality	职业 Occupation	备注 Note
17	Ted Hunter	41 岁 41	male 男	澳大利亚 Australia	教师 teacher	
18	Harrison William	50 岁 50	male 男	澳大利亚 Australia	商人 merchant	
备注 Note	住宿：2 个单间，3 个双人间，1 个家庭套房，3 个标间 Accommodation：2 single rooms，3 double rooms，1 suite for family，3 standard rooms					

根据上述两份表格的内容及导游服务工作要求，填写下列工作备忘信息。

Fill in the blanks of the working notes with the information from the above forms or in accordance with a guide's work requirements.

1. 旅行社信息

（1）地接社（local travel agency）：名称（name）＿＿＿＿＿＿＿

电话（phone）＿＿＿＿＿＿＿＿

（2）领队（tour leader）：姓名（name）＿＿＿＿＿＿

电话（phone）＿＿＿＿＿＿

（3）全导（national guide）：姓名（name）＿＿＿＿＿＿＿

电话（phone）＿＿＿＿＿＿

（4）北京地导（local guide in Beijing）：姓名（name）＿＿＿＿＿＿

电话（phone）＿＿＿＿＿＿

2. 旅游团成员信息

（1）游客人数（total number of tourists）＿＿＿＿＿＿＿，其中男（male）＿＿＿＿＿＿，女（female）＿＿＿＿＿，含儿童（child）＿＿＿＿＿。

（2）团队类型（team type）：独立团队（independent）□ 散客团队（individual）□

（3）客源地（origin country）＿＿＿＿＿＿＿＿＿＿

（4）使用语言（language）＿＿＿＿＿＿＿＿＿＿

3. 交通信息

（1）旅游团抵达信息（arrival information）：时间（time）＿＿＿＿＿地点（place）＿＿＿＿＿班次（flight）＿＿＿＿

（2）旅游团离开信息（departure information）：时间（time）＿＿＿＿＿＿

目的地(destination) _____ 班次(flight) _____

(3) 离开交通方式(departure transport means)：飞机(air)□　火车(train)□　汽车(coach)□

(4) 车辆信息(vehicle information)：车号(bus number) _____ 驾驶员姓名(driver's name) _____ 联系电话(phone) _____

(5) 订票方式(ticket reservation)：旅行社代订(by travel agency)□　游客自理(by tourists)□

(6) 车票变更(ticket change)：有(yes)□　无(no)□

4. 酒店房间信息

(1) 北京住宿酒店(name of the hotel in Beijing) _____

(2) 房间数(number of rooms) _____,其中,单间(single room) _____,双人间(double room) _____,家庭套房(suite for family) _____,标间(standard room) _____。

5. 餐饮信息

(1) 早餐类型(breakfast type)：自助餐(buffet)□　桌餐(table meal)□

(2) 中餐类型(lunch type)：自助餐(buffet)□　桌餐(table meal)□

(3) 正餐类型(dinner type)：自助餐(buffet)□　桌餐(table meal)□

(4) 用餐标准(meal standard)：中餐(lunch) _____ 正餐(dinner) _____

(5) 正餐是否含酒水(drinks in dinner)：有(yes)□　无(no)□

(6) 风味餐(flavor meal)：有(yes)□　无(no)□

(7) 餐饮禁忌(food taboo) _____

(8) 其他(other) _____

6. 游览信息

(1) 全程路线(travel route) _____

(2) 各地游览景点(main visiting places) _____

_____

_____

_____

(3) 自费项目(self-financed items)：有(yes)□　无(no)□

(4) 自费项目收费方式(charging method for self-financed items)：
组团社预收(charged by origin travel agency in advance)□
地接社现收(charged by local travel agency in cash)□

(5) 讲解要求(introduction requirement)_____

(6) 其他(others)：_____

7. 其他要求

(1) 其他会见、参观项目(other meeting, visiting arrangements)：有(yes)
□ 无(no)□

(2) 特殊关照对象(special attention)：残疾人(disabled)□ 病人
(patient)□

70 岁以上老人(70 years old and above)□ 儿童(child)□ 孕妇
(pregnant)□

(3) 需要特别准备的物品(special items to prepare)_____

实训项目 2　Task 2

情景对话：酒店房间预订确认

Dialogue：Reconfirmation of Hotel Reservation

实训要求：来自澳大利亚的 18 人旅游团 AU0606,在北京期间将入住北京香格里拉酒店。请以导游的身份,在旅游团入住前 6 小时,电话联系酒店前台,确认一周前预订的房间：2 个单人间、3 个双人间、1 个套房、3 个标准间,住 4 晚(6 月 6 日–9 日),并确认早餐形式(西餐、自助),告知对方客人到达酒店的大致时间。

Directions：The Australian tour group AU0606 of 18 persons will put up in Beijing Shangri-la Hotel during their stay in Beijing. You, the local guide, contact the hotel reception desk by telephone to reconfirm the room reservation made a week ago：2 single rooms, 3 double rooms, 1 suite, 3 standard rooms for 4 days(June 6–9). You also should confirm the breakfast service(buffet, western-style) and inform the hotel of the group's possible arrival time.

示例　Model

(G：local guide　R：hotel receptionist)

R：Beijing Shangri-la Hotel reception. May I help you?

G：Yes, I'm Jiang Min, local guide, from BJ ✳✳ Travel Service. I'd like to reconfirm our room reservation a week ago, for an Australian tour group of 18.

R：Just a minute. I'll check.... Oh, here is the reservation information. (Speaking slowly) 2 single rooms,3 double rooms, 1 suite, 3 standard rooms for 4 days, from June 6 to June 9. Is there any change?

G：Right! No change at all. I just want to reconfirm it.

R：Good! By the way, when will the group arrive at our hotel?

G：I'm afraid I can't tell you the exact time right now, but if everything is smooth, they will get to the hotel before 6 in the evening.

R：That's fine! We'll see you then.

G：I'd also like to confirm your breakfast service. Our tour group is from Australia. What they need is a buffet breakfast, Western-style.

R：No problem. Our hotel is an international one; it has a very good coffee shop, serving Western-style breakfast. I'm sure our Australian guests will like it.

G：Great! Thank you very much.

R：You are welcome.

参考答案 Key for Reference

实训项目 1　Task 1

1. 旅行社信息

(1) 地接社(local travel agency)：名称(name) __BJ ** Travel Service__
电话(phone) __010 - 53 ** 0062/158 ** 039599__

(2) 领队(tour leader)：姓名(name) __Mr. Ginpil__
电话(phone) __139 ** 743300__

(3) 全导(national guide)：姓名(name) __Mr. Lu Fan__
电话(phone) __133 ** 647643__

(4) 北京地导(local guide in Beijing)：姓名(name) __Mr. Jiang Min__
电话(phone) __136 ** 321369__

2. 旅游团成员信息

(1) 游客人数(total number of tourists) __18__ ，其中男(male) __10__ ，女(female) __8__ ，含儿童(child) __2__ 。

(2) 团队类型(team type)：独立团队(independent) ☑　散客团队(individual) □

(3) 客源地(origin country) __Australia__

(4) 使用语言(language) __English__

3．交通信息

（1）旅游团抵达信息（arrival information）：时间（time）　9：15 on June 6

地点（place）　Beijing（Capital International Airport）　　班次（flight）

CA1 **

（2）旅游团离开信息（departure information）：时间（time）　9：25 on June 10

目的地（destination）　Xi'an　班次（flight）　CA3 ***

（3）离开交通方式（departure transport means）：飞机（air）☑

火车（train）□　汽车（coach）□

（4）车辆信息（vehicle information）：

车号（bus number）　京B 33 ***

驾驶员姓名（driver's name）　Mr. Zhang Fu

联系电话（phone）　139 ** 473210

（5）订票方式（ticket reservation）：旅行社代订（by travel agency）☑

游客自理（by tourists）□

（6）车票变更（ticket changes）：有（yes）□　无（no）☑

4．酒店房间信息

（1）北京住宿酒店（name of the hotel in Beijing）　Beijing Shangri-la Hotel

（2）房间数（number of room）　9，其中，单间（single room）　2，双人间

（double room）　3，家庭套房（suite for family）　1，标间（standard

room）　3。

5．餐饮信息

（1）早餐类型（breakfast type）：自助餐（buffet）☑　桌餐（table meal）□

（2）中餐类型（lunch type）：自助餐（buffet）□　桌餐（table meal）☑

（3）正餐类型（dinner type）：自助餐（buffet）□　桌餐（table meal）☑

（4）用餐标准（meal standard）：中餐（lunch）　30RMB/person　　晚餐

（supper）　50RMB/person

（5）正餐是否含酒水（drinks in dinner）：有（yes）□　无（no）☑

（6）风味餐（flavor meal）：有（yes）□　无（no）☑

（7）餐饮禁忌（food taboo）　5 vegetarians

（8）其他（other）　nothing

6．游览信息

（1）全程路线（travel route）　Beijing-Xi'an-Nanjing-Shanghai

（2）各地游览景点（main visiting places）　Beijing：Tian'anmen Square,

Forbidden City, Panda Hall, Summer Palace, Great Wall, Ming Tombs, Temple of Heaven, Watch Beijing Opera; Xi'an: Museum of Qin Shi Huang Terracotta Warriors and Horses, City Wall, Big Wild Goose Pagoda, Muslim Quarter; Nanjing: Dr. Sun Yat-sen's Mausoleum, Ming Tomb, Linggu Temple, Hongshan Forest Zoo, Yangtze River Bridge, Presidential Palace, Qinhuai Scenic Zone, Confucius Temple

（3）自费项目（self-financed items）：有（yes）☑　无（no）□

（4）自费项目收费方式（charging method for self-financed items）：
组团社预收（charged by origin travel agency in advance）□
地接社现收（charged by local travel agency in cash）☑

（5）讲解要求（introduction requirement）<u>speak English fluently</u>

（6）其他（others）：<u>nothing</u>

7. 其他要求

（1）其他会见、参观项目（other meeting, visiting arrangements）：有（yes）□　无（no）☑

（2）特殊关照对象（special attention）：残疾人（disabled）□　病人（patient）☑　70 岁以上老人（70 years old and above）□　儿童（child）☑　孕妇（pregnant）□

（3）需要特别准备的物品（special items to prepare）：<u>nothing</u>

小贴士 Tips

导游上团前的心理准备

导游工作是脑力劳动，也是体力劳动。除了按照导游工作规范，热情地向游客提供基本的导游服务外，还要为需要特殊照顾的游客提供个性化服务。在接待工作中，有可能发生各种各样的问题或事故，需要导游去面对、解决。有时导游已经尽其可能向游客提供热情周到的服务，但由于其他接待环节出现差错或非人为因素造成旅游过程中的不愉快，也会导致游客的抱怨和投诉；甚至还有一些游客会无故挑剔或提出苛刻的要求。为此，导游必须有足够的心理准备，沉着冷静地面对意料之外的各种问题，并继续以自己的工作热情感化游客。

（胡华：《导游实务》，旅游教育出版社，2012 年。）

课后实训 After-class Practice

实训项目1 Task 1

实用写作：熟悉接待计划

Practical Writing：Study the Reception Plan

实训要求：现有来自美国纽约的24人旅游团，你是他们在北京期间的地接导游，旅行社提供了一份接待通知单（表1-3），要求认真准备，做好服务。阅读该接待通知单，准确掌握接待内容和要求，填写接待备忘信息。

Directions：Here is a tour group of 24 tourists from New York, USA. You will be their local guide during their stay in Beijing. The travel agency gives you a reception plan form（Form 1-3）as follows, and it demands your good preparation for serving the group. Study the given reception plan form, understand and grasp the task requirements, and make the working notes for your job.

表1-3　上海＊＊旅行社接待计划

Form 1-3　Reception Plan of SH＊＊ Travel Agency

组团单位 Organizing Agency	团号 Group Number	国籍 Nationality	游客人数 Number of Tourists	
上海＊＊旅行社 Shanghai ＊＊ Travel Agency	GLOTS－0205B	美国（纽约） USA（NY）	24人（男：13　女：11 儿童：0　老人：0 24（male：13 female：11 child：0 aged：0)	
抵达 **Arrival**	2016年9月10日18时25分 CZ51＊＊航班抵达首都机场 18：25 September 10, 2016 CZ51＊＊ PEK	**离开** **Departure**	2016年9月13日9时50分 CZ51＊＊离开首都机场 9：50 September 13, 2016 CZ51＊＊ PEK	
领队 **Leader**	王磊　Wang Lei　137＊＊733660			
住宿 **Hotel**	北京国际大饭店　11标准间,1单人间,加1全陪床 Beijing International Hotel 11 Standard Rooms, 1 Single Room, 1 National Guide Bed		**等级** **Standard**	4星级 4-star

续表

	日期 Date	早 Breakfast （自助餐 20 元/人） (buffet 20 RMB/person)		中 Lunch （桌餐 40 元/人） (table meal 40 RMB/person)		晚 Supper （桌餐 60 元/人） (table meal 60 RMB/person)	
		地点 place	标准 standard	地点 place	标准 standard	地点 place	标准 standard
餐饮 Meal	9 月 10 日 10th Sept					和平门 Heping Gate	便餐 light meal
	9 月 11 日 11th Sept	酒店 hotel	西式 western	长城 The Great Wall	便餐 light meal	全聚德 Quanjude	风味餐 local flavor
	9 月 12 日 12th Sept	酒店 hotel	西式 western	景江 Jingjiang	便餐 light meal	西苑 Xiyuan	便餐 light meal
	9 月 13 日 13th Sept	酒店 hotel	西式 western				

观光 Sight-seeing	9 月 10 日 10th Sept	机场接机；入住酒店；晚餐 airport pick-up, accommodation, supper
	9 月 11 日 11th Sept	长城；明十三陵；天安门；晚上观看京剧 Great Wall, Ming Tombs, Tian'anmen; watch Beijing Opera in the evening
	9 月 12 日 12th Sept	颐和园，天坛，故宫博物院；王府井夜市 Summer Palace, Temple of Heaven, Palace Museum; night fair at Wangfujing
	9 月 13 日 13th Sept	机场送机 airport see-off

派车单位 Coach Company	国旅车队 National Travel Team	车号 Bus Number	京 A06 ***	司机 Driver	李荣 Li Rong 139 ** 348901
行李车联络人 Luggage Contact	张师傅 Mr. Zhang 139 ** 609903				
旅行社联系电话 Travel Agency Tel	021 – 88 ** 9561	计调 Operator	周富 Zhou Fu 29 ** 6657	夜间电话 Night Service	139 ** 029873

备注 **Note**	1. 请导游与机场确认航班到达时间,并确认客人的回程机票。 Please call the airport to confirm the flight arrival time, and confirm the return tickets for tourists. 2. 西苑、长城、景江、全聚德的餐饮已订好,请导游约好开餐时间。 Meals at Xiyuan, the Great Wall, Jingjiang, and Quanjude have been reserved; please confirm the meal times. 3. 团队购物店为:北海水晶店、雅阁玉器店、名苑茶坊。 Group shopping: Beihai Crystal Shop, Yage Jade Shop, Mingyuan Tea Garden. 4. 9月11日晚的京剧入场券放在国际大酒店总台,请导游到总台领取。 The tickets for Beijing opera on the evening of September 11 are at the International Hotel. Get the tickets from the reception desk. 5. 此团为我社重点开线团,请导游做好导游服务工作,并注意餐饮质量。 This is our key line group. Make sure the guide service is good, and pay attention to the quality of the meals.
全导:张环 138＊＊900233 National Guide:Zhang Huan	地导:杨水灵 138＊＊889624 Local guide:Yang Shuiling

根据上述表格的内容及导游服务工作要求,填写下列工作备忘信息。

Fill in the blanks of the working notes with the information from the above form or in accordance with a guide's work requirements.

1. 旅行社信息

(1) 组团社(organizing travel agency):名称(name)＿＿＿＿＿＿＿＿＿

电话(phone)＿＿＿＿＿＿＿＿＿

(2) 领队(leader):姓名(name)＿＿＿＿＿＿＿＿＿＿

电话(phone)＿＿＿＿＿＿＿＿＿

(3) 全导(national guide):姓名(name)＿＿＿＿＿＿＿＿

电话(phone)＿＿＿＿＿＿＿＿＿

(4) 地导(local guide):姓名(name)＿＿＿＿＿＿＿＿＿＿

电话(phone)＿＿＿＿＿＿＿＿＿

2. 旅游团成员

(1) 游客人数(total number of tourists) ＿＿＿＿＿＿,其中男(male)＿＿＿＿＿＿,女(female)＿＿＿＿＿,老人(aged)＿＿＿＿＿,儿童(child)＿＿＿＿＿。

(2) 团队类型(team type):独立团队(independent)□ 散客团队

（individual）□

（3）客源地（origin country）＿＿＿＿＿＿

（4）使用语言（language）＿＿＿＿＿＿

3．交通

（1）旅游团抵达信息（arrival information）：时间（time）＿＿＿＿＿＿＿＿

　　地点（place）＿＿＿＿＿＿＿＿＿　　班次（flight）＿＿＿＿＿＿＿＿

（2）旅游团离开信息（departure information）：时间（time）＿＿＿＿＿＿＿

　　地点（place）＿＿＿＿＿＿＿＿＿　　班次（flight）＿＿＿＿＿＿＿＿

（3）离开交通方式（departure transport means）：飞机（air）□　火车（train）□　汽车（coach）□

（4）车辆信息（vehicle information）：车号（bus number）＿＿＿＿＿＿＿＿

　　驾驶员姓名（driver's name）＿＿＿＿＿＿　联系电话（phone）＿＿＿＿＿＿

（5）订票方式（ticket reservation）：旅行社代订（by agent）□　游客自理（by tourists）□

（6）车票变更（ticket changes）：有（yes）□　无（no）□

4．酒店房间

（1）住宿酒店（name of the hotel）＿＿＿＿＿＿＿＿＿＿＿＿＿

（2）房间数（number of rooms）＿＿＿＿＿＿＿＿，其中，单人间（single room）＿＿＿＿＿＿＿＿，标准间（standard room）＿＿＿＿＿＿＿＿，双人间（double room）＿＿＿＿＿＿＿＿，商务套间（business suite）＿＿＿＿＿＿＿＿，全陪床（national guide bed）＿＿＿＿＿＿＿＿。

5．餐饮

（1）早餐类型（breakfast type）：自助餐（buffet）□　桌餐（table meal）□

（2）中餐类型（lunch type）：自助餐（buffet）□　桌餐（table meal）□

（3）晚餐类型（supper type）：自助餐（buffet）□　桌餐（table meal）□

（4）用餐标准（meal standard）：中餐（lunch）＿＿＿＿＿＿＿＿

　　晚餐（supper）＿＿＿＿＿＿＿＿

（5）是否含酒水（drinks in meal）：有（yes）□　无（no）□

（6）风味餐（flavor meal）：有（yes）□　无（no）□

（7）餐饮禁忌（food taboo）＿＿＿＿＿＿＿＿＿

（8）其他（other）＿＿＿＿＿＿＿＿＿

6．游览

（1）全程路线（travel route）＿＿＿＿＿＿＿＿

（2）主要参观游览景点（main visiting places）_____

（3）自费项目（self-financed items）：有（yes）☐　无（no）☐

（4）自费项目收费方式（charging method for self-financed items）：

　　组团社预收（charged by organizing travel agency in advance）☐

　　地接社现收（charged by local travel agency in cash）☐

（5）讲解要求（orientation requirements）_____

（6）其他（others）_____

7. 其他要求

（1）其他会见、参观项目（other meeting, visiting arrangements）：有（yes）
　　☐　无（no）☐

（2）特殊关照对象（special attention）：残疾人（disabled）☐　70 岁以上
　　老人（70 years old and above）☐　儿童（child）☐　孕妇（pregnant）☐
　　病人（patient）☐

（3）需要特别准备的物品（special items to prepare）：_____

实训项目2　Task 2

情景对话：饭店订餐确认

Dialogue：Reconfirmation of Meal Reservation

实训要求：来自中国上海的24人旅游团，在北京期间的9月11日晚将在全聚德王府井店用餐。请以导游杨水灵的身份，在当天电话联系饭店前台，确认一周前的预订：6桌，每桌1000元，并告知对方客人到达饭店的大致时间。

Directions：The tour group of 24 from Shanghai, will have dinner at Quanjude Roast Duck Restaurant (Wangfujing Branch)on the evening of September 11. You (Yang Shuiling), the local guide, contact the restaurant reception desk by telephone to reconfirm the meal reservation made a week ago：6 tables, 1000 yuan per table. You also inform them of the possible arrival time of the group.

示例　Model

（G：local guide　R：restaurant receptionist）

R：Good Morning, this is Quanjude Restaurant, Wangfujing Branch. Can I help you?

G：This is Yang speaking. I made a reservation for this evening. I ordered 24 portions of Beijing Roast Duck and spring rolls.

R：OK, can I have your full name please?

G：Sure, Yang Shuiling.

R：Let me check, hold on please. Good, you've ordered meals for 24 persons under the name of Yang. Is that right?

G：Yes, that's it. I ordered 6 tables in all for 24 persons, 1000 RMB each table.

R：All right. Can I check your phone number?

G：No problem. 138 ** 889624.

R：I see, thank you. One more thing, what time would the guests come?

G：Well, around 6.

R：Good! We look forward to having you with us! Have a nice day!

G：You too. Bye.

参考答案 Key for Reference

实训项目1　Task 1

1. 旅行社信息

(1) 组团社(organizing travel agency)：名称(name)　Shanghai ** Travel Agency　电话(phone)　021 - 88 ** 9561

(2) 领队(leader)：姓名(name)　Mr. Wang Lei
电话(phone)　137 ** 733660

(3) 全导(national guide)：姓名(name)　Zhang Huan
电话(phone)　138 ** 900233

(4) 地导(local guide)：姓名(name)　Yang Shuiling
电话(phone)　138 ** 889624

2. 旅游团成员

(1) 游客人数(total number of tourists)　24　,其中男(male)　13　,女(female)　11　,老人(aged)　0　,儿童(child)　0　。

(2) 团队类型(team type)：独立团队(independent)　☑　散客团队(individual)　□

(3) 客源地(origin country)　USA

(4) 使用语言(language)　English

3．交通

（1）旅游团抵达信息（arrival information）：时间（time）<u>18：25 September 10, 2016</u> 地点（place）<u>Beijing Capital International Airport</u> 班次（flight）<u>CZ51 **</u>

（2）旅游团离开信息（departure information）：时间（time）<u>9：50 September 13th, 2016</u> 地点（place）<u>Beijing Capital International Airport</u> 班次（flight）<u>CZ51 **</u>

（3）离开交通方式（departure transport means）：飞机（air）☑ 火车（train）□ 汽车（coach）□

（4）车辆信息（vehicle information）：车号（bus number）<u>京 A06 ***</u>
驾驶员姓名（driver's name）<u>Li Rong</u>
联系电话（phone）<u>139 ** 348901</u>

（5）订票方式（ticket reservation）：旅行社代订（by agent）☑ 游客自理（by tourists）□

（6）车票变更（ticket changes）：有（yes）□ 无（no）☑

4．酒店房间

（1）住宿酒店（name of the hotel）<u>Beijing International Hotel</u>

（2）房间数（number of rooms）<u>13</u>，其中，单人间（single room）<u>1</u>，标准间（standard room）<u>11</u>，双人间（double room）<u>0</u>，商务套间（business suite）<u>0</u>，全陪床（national guide bed）<u>1</u>。

5．餐饮

（1）早餐类型（breakfast type）：自助餐（buffet）☑ 桌餐（table meal）□

（2）中餐类型（lunch type）：自助餐（buffet）□ 桌餐（table meal）☑

（3）晚餐类型（supper type）：自助餐（buffet）□ 桌餐（table meal）☑

（4）用餐标准（meal standard）：中餐（lunch）<u>40</u> 晚餐（supper）<u>60</u>

（5）是否含酒水（drinks in meal）：有（yes）□ 无（no）☑

（6）风味餐（flavor meal）：有（yes）☑ 无（no）□

（7）餐饮禁忌（food taboo）<u>no</u>

（8）其他（other）<u>nothing</u>

6．游览

（1）全程路线（travel route）<u>Beijing</u>

（2）主要参观游览景点（main visiting places）：<u>Great Wall, Ming Tombs, Tian'anmen, watch Beijing Opera, Summer Palace, Temple of Heaven,</u>

<u>Palace Museum, night fair at Wangfujing</u>

（3）自费项目（self-financed items）：有（yes）☑ 无（no）□

（4）自费项目收费方式（charging method for self-financed items）：

组团社预收（charged by organizing travel agency in advance）□

地接社现收（charged by local travel agency in cash）☑

（5）讲解要求（introduction requirements） <u>speak English</u>

（6）其他（others） <u>nothing</u>

7．其他要求

（1）其他会见、参观项目（other meeting, visiting arrangements）：有（yes）
□ 无（no）☑

（2）特殊关照对象（special attention）：残疾人（disabled）□ 70 岁以上
老人（70 years old and above□ 儿童（child）□ 孕妇（pregnant）□
病人（patient）□

（3）需要特别准备的物品（special items to prepare）：<u>nothing</u>

语言储备 Words and Expressions

1．专业术语 Special Terms

reception plan/program	接待计划
service item	服务项目
itinerary	旅游行程
origin country	客源国
tour group	旅游团
travel/tour route	旅游线路
group No.	团号
way of payment	结算方式
package tour	包价旅游
wonder travel service	豪华旅游服务
serial number	序号
arrival time	抵达时间
departure time	出发时间
tourist activity	旅游活动
tour leader/tour escort	领队

scenic spot	景点
sightseeing	游览
entertainment	娱乐
tourism administration/authority	旅游局
guide book	旅游指南
holiday inn	假日酒店
travel agency/service	旅行社
escorted tour	全程陪同旅游
national guide	全程导游,全导,全陪
local(tour) guide	地接导游,地导,地陪
off-peak season	淡季
peak season	旺季

2. 实用句型　Useful Sentences

(1) I am from MEL ** Travel Service.

我是 MEL ** 旅行社的。

(2) May I know the name of the tour group?

请问您的旅游团名称是什么?

(3) It's a group of 16 tourists, 9 males and 7 females.

本团共 16 名旅客,9 男 7 女。

(4) Here is the reception plan for the tour group AU0606.

这是 AU0606 旅游团的接待计划。

(5) Is there any special service requirement?

有什么特殊服务要求吗?

(6) Our flight is delayed(on schedule).

我们的航班晚点(正点)。

(7) I'd like to confirm(reconfirm) the hotel reservation for our tour group.

我想(再)确认一下我们旅游团预订的房间。

(8) I'd like to check the meal reservation.

我想核实一下我们的订餐。

(9) The Australian group will arrive at the airport at 2: 00 p. m.

澳洲团将在下午 2 点抵达机场。

(10) So let's meet at the airport parking lot on time.

我们准时在机场停车场见。

(11) —How much is the tour?

团费多少?

—2,000 yuan for each person.

每人2,000元。

—What does it include?

包含哪些费用?

—It includes your air fare, hotel accommodations and meals.

包含飞机票、食宿。

(12) Breakfast is included in the room rate.

房费含早餐。

知识链接 Related Knowledge

导游分类

1. 按工作区域划分,导游可分为:海外领队、全程陪同导游人员(简称"全导"或"全陪")、地方陪同导游人员(简称"地导"或"地陪")、景区景点导游人员。

2. 按语种划分,导游可分为:中文导游(包括普通话、方言、少数民族语导游)和外文导游。外文导游分为常用语种导游和非常用语种导游。常用语种主要包括英语、法语、韩语、日语、俄语、德语;非常用语种主要包括两个语种群:一是欧洲语系,主要有西班牙语、葡萄牙语、捷克语、阿尔巴尼亚语、波兰语、塞尔维亚语等;二是亚非语系,主要有阿拉伯语、朝鲜语、印尼语、越南语、马来语、缅甸语、泰国语、僧迦罗语、豪萨语、斯瓦希里语等。

3. 按技术等级划分,导游可分为:初级导游、中级导游、高级导游、特级导游。

导游员素质要求

1. 政治素质

导游员应热爱祖国,遵纪守法,恪守职业道德,自觉维护国家利益、民族尊严及旅游者和旅行社的合法权益,自觉抵制团队运作过程中的违规违法行为。

2. 思想素质

导游员应有优秀的道德品质和高尚的情操,讲文明,遵守社会公德,尽职敬业,为旅游者提供热情周到的服务,完成旅游接待计划所规定的各项任务,按照旅游合同的约定兑现旅游服务。

3. 技能素质

(1)语言能力。导游员应具备过硬的语言表达能力、娴熟的导游讲解技巧和强烈的礼貌语言使用意识。

(2)接待操作能力。导游员应符合法定的上岗资质,并具备独立工作能力、组织协调能力、人际交往能力和应急问题处理能力。

(3)知识要求。导游员应掌握法津法规常识、旅行常识、政治经济和社会知识、旅游地历史、地理、文化和民俗、景点景观等方面的知识及心理学和美学知识。

4. 心理素质

导游员应心胸开阔、善解人意、耐心细致,并具有良好的观察能力和感知能力、调整旅游者情绪的能力、自我心理平衡能力、承受能力及沉着冷静和有条不紊的处事能力。

5. 身体素质

导游员应具有健康的体魄和充沛的体力。

6. 职业形象

(1)仪容仪表。导游员应仪表端庄,按照旅行社的要求着装。服装要整洁、大方、得体。

(2)仪态。导游员应表情稳重自然,态度和蔼诚恳,富有亲和力,言行有度,举止符合礼仪规范。

7. 继续教育

导游员应参加继续教育培训学习(尤其是相关应急预案培训),不断提高自己的业务知识水平和操作技能。

8. 职业等级

导游员的职业等级是导游服务能力的标记,导游应通过不断学习和实操锻炼,通过考核获得更高的职业等级资质。

(中华人民共和国国家标准:《导游服务规范 GB/T 15971—2010》。)

模块二　接团服务

Module 2　Meeting on Arrival

任务描述 Task Description

　　接团服务是指导游在旅游团抵达后从机场、车站或码头到下榻酒店的转移途中要做的工作。导游员的接团服务主要包括认找旅游团、迎接旅游者（致欢迎辞）。

Tour group meeting service refers to the work the tour guide does at the airport, railway station, bus station or port and on the way to the hotel after the tour group arrives. It includes recognizing the tour group and welcoming the tourists(delivering a welcome speech).

任务目标 Learning Objectives

　　1. 掌握接团准备的主要内容和接团服务的标准流程；掌握辨识旅游团的方法；能够熟练地进行旅游团辨识操作；掌握相关的基本用语和表达。

Be familiar with the preparative work and the standard procedures of the tour group meeting service. Master the methods of recognizing tour groups and be able to recognize tour groups quickly. Use the words and expressions concerned freely in communication.

　　2. 能够专业化地实施旅游团接待程序；使用英语与外国旅游团交流,开展接待工作。

Work expertly following the procedures of receiving tour groups. Communicate in English with foreign tour group in reception.

　　3. 培养耐心细致的工作作风,良好的服务意识、合作意识和团队意识。

Develop a good habit of working patiently and carefully, and a strong consciousness of service, cooperation and team work.

工作流程 Working Process

1. 阅读接待计划，了解团队情况。旅游团抵达之前认真阅读接待计划和有关资料，准确地了解旅游团的服务项目和要求，对重要事宜做好记录。

Before a tour group arrives, read the tour reception plan and other relevant materials carefully so as to know well about all services and requirements of the group, and make notes of important matters.

2. 与计调交接。与计调联系，落实、核查旅游团的交通、食宿、行李运输等事宜。

Contact the operator of the travel service. Check the arrangements concerning transport, accommodation, luggage, etc. of the tour group.

3. 做好物质准备。接团前做好必要的物质准备，带好接待计划、导游证、导游旗、接站牌、餐厅或酒店的确认件等物品资料，为 10 人以上团队配备扩音设备。

Make good preparations before leaving for the pick-up. Take along the reception plan, tour guide's identity certificate, guide flag, sign board, confirmation letters of restaurants and hotels, and a loudspeaker if there are more than 10 persons in the group.

4. 确认旅游团抵达时间。在接站出发前确认旅游团所乘交通工具及准确抵达时间，并与全程导游保持联络。

Before leaving to meet the tour group, confirm the transport means and the exact arrival time of the group and keep contact with the national guide.

5. 迎接旅游团。

Meet the tour group.

（1）手举标牌，站在机场到达大厅出口处的醒目位置。

Stand in an obvious place at the exit of the Airport Arrivals Lounge by holding a sign board with the name of the tour group on it.

① 根据不同国籍人的特征、衣着、组团社的徽记等辨识旅游团。

Spot the group according to the characteristics of nationality, clothes, the logo of the tour organizing agency, etc.

② 及时与领队、全程导游接洽，核对旅游团的国别（或地区）、人数、客源

地组团社的名称、领队和全程导游的姓名等。

Contact the tour group leader and the national guide and check the nationality (or region), the number of the group, the name of the tour organizing agency and the names of the tour group leader and the national guide.

（2）尽快与领队、全程导游核实旅游团确切人数,明确人数有没有变化。

Verify the actual number of the tour group members with the tour leader or the national guide as soon as possible and check if there is any change in the actual number of the group members.

6. 集中清点行李。

Make sure the tourists get all their luggage at a designated place, count the pieces of luggage if necessary.

7. 集合登车。

Gather and get on the coach.

（1）提醒游客带齐随身物品,引导他们前往乘车处。

Remind the tourists to take all their belongings and take them to the coach.

（2）在车门旁恭候,协助登车,做到礼貌得体,同时识记游客。

Stand by the coach to assist tourists to get on the coach politely and get familiar with the tourists in the meantime.

（3）协助游客入座,帮助游客放置随身行李。

Assist the tourists to be seated, and to put away their carry-on bags.

（4）礼貌地清点人数,到齐坐稳后请司机开车。

Count heads in a polite way to make sure every tourist is on the coach and seated before the coach sets off.

8. 致欢迎辞。车辆启动、运行平稳后,导游致欢迎辞。

Make a welcome speech when the bus runs steadily.

（1）问候游客。

Greet the group.

（2）表示欢迎。

Extend a warm welcome.

（3）介绍自己和同事。

Introduce yourself and your workmate(s).

（4）表达为游客服务的意愿。

Express willingness to serve the guests.

（5）表达祝愿。

Express wishes.

小贴士 Tips

北京首都国际机场航站楼及相对应的航空公司

T1 即 1 号航站楼,对应的航空公司有：CN 大新华;JD 北京首都;HU 海南国内航班;GS 天津;9C 春秋;8L 云南祥鹏;FU 福州。

T2 即 2 号航站楼,对应的航空公司有：7J 塔吉克;PS 乌克兰国际;7C 济州;NS 河北;2D 美国动力;J2 阿塞拜疆;Y7 俄罗斯北方之星;R3 俄罗斯雅库特;D7 亚洲;HZ 俄罗斯奥罗拉;5J 菲律宾宿务太平洋;FM 上海;DL 美国达美;CZ 中国南方;OQ 重庆;HU 海南国际航班;MU 中国东方;MF 厦门;KE 大韩;AF 法国;SU 俄罗斯;HY 乌兹别克斯坦;KL 荷兰皇家;KC 阿斯塔纳;JS 朝鲜;PK 巴基斯坦;GA 印度尼西亚鹰;IR 伊朗;UL 斯里兰卡;T5 土库曼斯坦;VN 越南;DT 安哥拉;AH 阿尔及利亚;HX 香港;LV 马尔代夫美佳环球。

T3 即 3 号航站楼,对应的航空公司有：DZ 东海;HM 塞舌尔;KY 昆明;IA 伊拉克;W5 伊朗马汉;GJ 浙江长龙;QW 青岛;HA 夏威夷;TV 西藏;GH 俄罗斯;MK 毛里求斯;LO 波兰;CA 中国国际;LX 瑞士;CA 大连;SC 山东;3U 四川;OS 奥地利;SK 北欧;LH 德意志汉莎;OZ 韩亚;AC 加拿大;UA 美国;NH 全日空;TK 土耳其;MS 埃及;TG 泰国;SQ 新加坡;AY 芬兰;CX 国泰;BA 英国;JL 日本;KA 港龙;EK 阿联酋;LY 以色列;QR 卡塔尔;S7 俄罗斯西伯利亚;NX 澳门;CI 中华;EY 阿联酋阿提哈德;BR 长荣;ZH 深圳;OM 蒙古;U6 乌拉尔;AA 美国;UN 俄罗斯洲际;ET 埃塞俄比亚;PR 菲律宾;MH 马来西亚;HO 上海吉祥。

课堂实训 In-class Practice

实训项目1 Task 1

情景对话：*认找旅游团*

Dialogue：Recognize a Tour Group

实训要求：掌握辨识旅游团的程序和基本方法；能够熟练进行旅游团认找；能熟练使用英语开展接待工作。

Directions：Grasp the general procedures and methods of recognizing a tour group and be able to recognize a tour group quickly. Provide good meeting service with English as the working language.

实训材料：接站牌、导游旗、模拟机场大厅广播播报、接站交通车。

Props：sign board, guide flag, broadcasting of Airport Arrivals Lounge, transport vehicle

实训步骤 Steps

第一步：学生分组扮演地接导游、领队、全程导游、游客、乘客。

Step 1：Divide the class into groups to play the roles of local guide, tour leader, national guide, tourists and passengers.

第二步：准备接站牌、导游旗和机场到达大厅广播播报。

Step 2：Prepare the receiving board (sign), guide flag and broadcasting of announcement at the Airport Arrivals Lounge.

第三步：持接站牌等候。

Step 3：Wait holding up the receiving board (sign).

第四步：认找旅游团。认找的方法有两种：① 地接导游持或举接站牌在出口醒目位置等候；② 根据旅游计划材料和游客信息主动上前认找。

Step 4：Recognize the tour group. There are two methods：① step up to recognize according to the tour plan and tourist information；② wait holding up the board at an obvious position of the exit.

示例 Model

Method 1

（G：local guide, Mr. Jiang Min P：passenger L：tour leader, Mr. Ginpil）

（Tour guide Mr. Jiang Min is waiting for a tour group from Australia at the exit of the Airport Arrivals Lounge. To avoid missing the group, he is holding up a sign board with the name of the group on it. He steps to a gentleman coming out.）

G：Excuse me, are you Mr. Ginpil from Australia?

P：No, my last name is White.

G：I'm so sorry.

P：Never mind.

G：(seeing another man) Excuse me, are you Mr. Ginpil, the tour leader of the "Australian cultural tour group"?

L：Yes, I am.

G：Oh, nice to meet you, Mr. Ginpil. Welcome to Beijing. I am Jiang Min from Beijing ＊＊ Travel Service. I'll be your tour guide during your stay in Beijing.

L：Nice to meet you, Mr. Jiang.

（易玉婷,汪锋:《英语导游实务——导游业务部分》,国防工业出版社, 2012 年。)

Method 2

（G：local guide, Mr. Jiang Min　T：tourist, Miss Parker）

（At the airport, the tour guide Mr. Jiang Min, meets his tour group from the US. He is holding up a welcome sign with Miss Parker's name and her company's name on it. ）

T：Hello, you must be Mr. Jiang, our local guide?

G：Oh, yes. I'm Jiang Min with BJ ＊＊ Travel service. Nice to meet you, Miss Parker. Welcome to China.

T：Nice to meet you, too. Thank you for coming to meet us.

G：It's my pleasure. We've been looking forward to your visit. How was your flight? It's such a long journey.

T：Not too bad. A little bit tired. Mrs. Smith was airsick.

G：Is she all right now? We have medicine for airsickness.

T：That'd be good.

G：Well, I hope you'll have a pleasant stay here.

T：Thank you. I'm sure we will.

G：Hello, everyone. My name is Jiang Min. I'll be your tour guide. It's nice to see you. Our bus is waiting outside the airport. Mrs. Smith, I hope you feel better after you take the medicine. Shall we go now?

T：OK.

G：Please follow me.

（郑毅,郑雪梅:《旅游英语视听说》,外语教学与研究出版社,2014 年。)

实训项目2　Task 2

情景演讲：致欢迎辞

Speech：A Welcome Speech

实训要求：掌握英语欢迎辞的要求、内容和语言风格；准备一份欢迎辞,反复进行口头练习。

Directions：Master what an English welcome speech is：the structure, the content, the speaking style and so on. Prepare such a speech and practice.

示例　Model

Good morning, ladies and gentlemen!

Welcome to Beijing! We're heading for our hotel. First of all, let me introduce myself and my colleague to you. I'm Jiang Min, your tour guide during your stay in Beijing. My English name is Jack. You can just call me Jack or Mr. Jiang. This is Mr. Zhang Fu, our driver. He has been driving for our travel service for more than 20 years; he is a very good driver. We're with Beijing ** Travel Service. On behalf of the travel service, I'd like to extend a warm welcome to all of you.

During your stay in Beijing, I shall do my best to offer you the best guiding service and make your trip a pleasant and happy one. If you have any problems or need my help, please don't hesitate to let me know. As an old Chinese saying goes, "Isn't it delightful to have friends from afar?" May all of us become good friends.

Beijing is the capital city of China and also a famous historic and cultural city with a long history. There are many well-known tourist spots which attract tourists from home and abroad. The Great Wall, the Forbidden City, the Temple of Heaven, the Summer Palace and Tian'anmen Square are worth visiting. Other tourist spots such as the Beihai Park, Beijing Hutong and the ruins of Peking Man at Zhoukoudian are high up on the list. Now I'd like to introduce tomorrow's travel schedule to you. I hope you would like it.

At 8：00 a. m. , we'll begin our fantastic tour in Beijing. The first scenic spot we'll visit is Tian'anmen Square, where you can see many famous buildings in Beijing. Then, we shall visit the Forbidden City, the largest palace museum in

China. At 7：00 in the evening, we'll watch Beijing Opera（京剧）at the theater.

You're going to stay at Beijing Shangri-la Hotel, a luxurious, five-star hotel. This afternoon, you are free and you may go around the city nearby the hotel. Since it is the first time for you to travel in Beijing, you'd better not go out or travel alone. In case you get lost or have other troubles, call me. My mobile phone number is 136＊＊321369.

It takes us about fifty minutes to get to the hotel. You may have a rest now. Thank you for your attention！

小贴士 Tips

接团致欢迎辞

致欢迎辞一般应在游客上车后、车子到达饭店前进行。如果旅游团人数很多,需分乘几辆车运送,每辆车又不能保证各有一位陪同,那么这种情况下在机场(车站)致欢迎辞比较好。

致欢迎辞时,导游应面对游客,站在车厢的前部,司机的附近。若乘坐的是小型旅游车,可以坐着,但要侧身面对游客,这样便于互动。致欢迎辞时,身体不可摇摆抖动,不要把手插在裤兜、衣兜里,或做不协调的动作。

欢迎辞的基本内容:

问候语:礼貌问候,如"各位来宾、各位朋友,大家好！大家辛苦了……";

欢迎语:代表所在旅行社、本人及司机欢迎游客光临本地;

介绍语:介绍自己的姓名及所属单位,介绍司机;

希望语:表示提供服务的诚挚愿望、希望得到合作的意愿;

祝愿语:预祝旅游顺利、愉快;

本地介绍:介绍本地概况,如地理位置、历史沿革、人口状况、行政区的划分、市政建设、风光风情、当地的天气及交通情况等。

(袁银枝:《导游业务》,中国轻工业出版社,2012年。)

课后实训 After-class Practice

实训项目 Task

实用制作：制作接站牌。

DIY：Making a receiving sign/board.

实训要求：掌握制作接站牌的基本方法。

Directions：Master the methods of making a receiving sign/board.

实训材料：硬纸板、纸张、记号笔、蜡笔或水彩笔、胶水或双面胶

Props：cardboard, paper, marker pen, crayon or water color pen, glue or sticky tape

实训步骤 Steps

第一步：裁剪硬板纸,尺寸：不小于45cm×30cm。

Step 1：Cut the cardboard to the size no smaller than 45cm×30cm.

第二步：在一张相同大小的纸上打印或书写旅游团的名称(团号)或领队的姓名等,字体要醒目、美观。

Step 2：Print or write information, such as the name (code) of the tour group or the name of the group leader, on a piece of paper (the same size of the cardboard). Be sure the printing or writing should be clear and good-looking.

第三步：把打印(写)好的纸贴在硬板纸上。

Step 3：Paste or stick the printed(written) paper on the cardboard.

示例1　Model 1

> Welcome
> 　　Australia Cultural
> 　Tour Group AU0606

示例 2　Model 2

> Welcome
> 　Mr. Ginpil
> 　　from Australia

语言储备 Words and Expressions

1. 专业术语 Special Terms

scenic-spot guide	景点导游
professional tour guide	专职导游
part-time tour guide	兼职导游
international tour guide	国际导游
domestic tour guide	国内导游
foreign language-speaking tour guide	外语导游
Putonghua/Mandarin-speaking tour guide	普通话导游
junior/intermediate guide	初级/中级导游
senior guide	高级导游
tour organizing agency	组团社
local tour/travel agency/service	地接社
tour/travel agency/service	旅行社
tour/travel agent	旅行代理商
post-arrival service	抵达后的服务
scenic spot ticket	景点门票
parking lot	停车场

2. 实用句型 Useful Sentences

（1）Excuse me, you are Mr. Cooper from Australia, aren't you?

　　打扰一下,请问您是来自澳大利亚的库珀先生吗?

（2）Did you have a pleasant flight?

　　旅行很愉快吧?

（3）My name is Chen Hui, from Beijing ** Travel Service. I'll be your tour guide today as you go around Beijing.

我叫陈惠,来自北京＊＊旅行社,我将是您今天在北京游玩时的导游。

(4) I'm Lu Yang, your guide. It's nice to have you all with us.

我是陆洋,你们的导游。能和大家在一起太好了。

(5) My name is Alice. I'll be accompanying you on your sightseeing tour today.

我叫爱丽丝,我会陪同您进行今天的观光。

(6) Please allow me to introduce Mr. Xu to you. He is the general manager of our travel agency.

请允许我向您介绍徐先生,他是我们旅行社的总经理。

(7) May I introduce Mr. Zhang to you, our driver on this trip?

让我介绍一下我们旅行社的司机张先生。

(8) May I have the pleasure of introducing my workmate to you? This is our local guide Jiang Min from BJ ＊＊ Travel Service.

请允许我向你们介绍一下我的同事,这是北京＊＊旅行社的地接导游姜敏。

(9) I'm very glad to have this opportunity to meet you.

很高兴有机会见到你。

(10) I'm very pleased to make your acquaintance.

很高兴认识你。

(11) It's my honor to meet you, Mr. Miller.

米勒先生,很荣幸见到您。

知识链接 Related Knowledge

航空旅行知识

1. 航班、班次

民航的运输飞行主要有三种形式:班期飞行、加班飞行和包机飞行。其中,班期飞行是按照班期时刻表和规定的航线,定机型、定日期、定时刻的飞行;加班飞行是根据临时需要在班期飞行以外增加的飞行;包机飞行则是按照包机单位的要求,在现有航线上或以外进行的专用飞行。

航班分为定期航班和不定期航班。前者是指飞机定期自始发站起飞,按照规定的航线经过经停站至终点站,或直接到达终点站的航班。在国际航线上飞行的航班被称为国际航班,在国内航线上飞行的航班被称为国内航班。航班又分为去程航班和回程航班。为方便运输和用户使用,每个航班均编有航班号。中国国际航班的航班号是由执行该航班任务的航空公司的二字代码和3个阿拉伯数字组成,其中最后一个数字为奇数的表示去程航班,最后一个数字为偶数的则表示回程航班。例如CA982指中国国际航空公司承担的自纽约至北京的国际航班。中国国内航班的航班号由执行该航任务的航空公司的二字代码和4个阿拉伯数字组成,其中第一位数字表示执行该航班任务的航空公司或所属管理局,第二位数字表示该航班终点站所属的管理局,第三、四位数字表示班次及该航班的具体编号。其中,第四位数字若为奇数,则表示该航班为去程航班;若为偶数,则为回程航班。例如CA1201表示由中国国际航空公司承担飞行任务的由北京至西安的去程航班。又如,MU5302指东方航空公司承担飞行任务的由广州至上海的回程航班。

班次是指在单位时间内(通常用一个星期计算)飞行的航班数(包括去程航班与回程航班),班次是根据注返量需求与运能来确定的。

2. 客舱等级

国际航空运输中通常用英文字母表示客舱等级。

F 表示头等舱(First Class)

C 表示公务舱(Business Class)

Y 表示经济舱(Economy Class)

K 表示平价舱(Thrift)

3. 机场建设费

证收机场建设费于1980年在北京一地试行,1981年在全国推开,开始是面向出境国际旅客证收,后为了建立旅游发展基金,证收对象扩展到除下述旅客外的所有离境旅客:在国内机场中转未出隔离厅的国际旅客;乘坐国际航班出境,乘坐香港、澳门地区航班出港的持外交护照的旅客;持半票的12周岁以下的儿童;乘坐国内航班在当日(与机票所到的下一航班起飞时间间隔8小时以内)中转的旅客。自2004年9月1号起,机场建设费并入机票中,旅客退票时机场建设费要一并退还,并在退款单中单列,不收退票手续费。

4. 民航发展基金

乘坐飞机需要缴纳一定的民航发展基金。国内航线为每人次50元,国际航线为每人次90元。

(叶娅丽:《导游业务规程与技巧》,北京出版社,2012年。)

模块三　商讨行程

Module 3　Itinerary Discussion

任务描述 Task Description

核对、修改、商定行程是旅游团抵达后开始游览前和游览中的重要工作程序。旅游团抵达后,地接导游应与领队、全程导游一起核对、商定旅行社已经安排好的旅游团行程,这也是地接导游和领队、全程导游之间合作的开始。在旅游过程中,因情况的变化,导游也常需要与领队、游客商量调整行程。

It is an important step to discuss, modify and confirm the itinerary with the tour group. Upon the group's arrival, the local guide must discuss and confirm the itinerary made by the travel agency together with the tour leader and the national guide, which is also the beginning of the cooperation between them. In the course of tour, it is often the case that the itinerary has to be adjusted because of unexpected happenings.

任务目标 Learning Objectives

1. 了解核对日程的主要内容、修改日程的主要情形及其原因; 掌握商谈时的常用语和表达。

Know what itinerary confirmation is, and why and how itinerary modification is made. Master words and expressions used in the talk of itinerary confirmation and modification.

2. 熟练地与领队、全程导游核对日程,合理修改和调整日程; 了解行程的哪些方面需要与领队和全程导游确认。

Be able to discuss the itinerary with the tour leader, the national guide, understanding the principles of adjusting itinerary, and to modify or adjust it upon request. Know what aspects of the itinerary should be confirmed with the tour leader and the national guide.

3. 培养善于沟通的职业素养；培养良好的服务意识、团队意识和合作意识。

Learn how to communicate with others; develop service consciousness, team spirit and cooperation initiative.

工作流程 Working Process

1. 向领队和全陪出示初步行程，并与他们进行商讨。

Present the preliminary itinerary to the tour leader and the national guide, and discuss it with them.

（1）征求领队对由地接导游代表地接社草拟的行程安排的意见。

Ask for opinions of the tour leader about the preliminary itinerary drafted by the local guide on behave of the receiving travel agency.

（2）核实游客在各地逗留的天数、计划参观的景点名称、在这些景点的时间分布。

Check and confirm the number of the days that the tour group stays in each city, the names of the scenic spots to be visited and the time distribution for them.

（3）核实每日具体日程安排。

Verify the detailed daily schedule arrangements.

（4）确认特殊活动安排。

Confirm the arrangements of special activities.

（5）明确离开该地的车辆、航班、火车班次及时间。

Confirm the transport means, the flight or train number and its time for departure in each city.

（6）向领队询问关于自费活动安排的建议。

Ask for the tour leader's opinion about arranging self-paying items.

（7）商量领队和全程导游提出的其他建议或要求。

Discuss other suggestions given by the tour leader or the national guide if any.

2. 如果遇有需要修改（变更）活动计划和日程的情况或要求，要根据情形，采取相应的处理方法。

If there is a request or necessity of change in the itinerary, adopt different solutions for different situations.

（1）不涉及日程或接待标准太大变化的变更意见或要求

suggestions or requests that do not result in big change of the schedule or the reception costs

① 如果没有额外费用、对原计划没有大的影响，可以同意。

If there are no extra costs and no big impact on the original schedule, give consent to the request.

② 如果有额外费用，该费用必须按规定予以计算，并进行收取。

If there are extra costs, the fees must be added and collected according to the provision.

（2）涉及日程变化或接待标准变化的变更意见或要求

suggestions or requests that result in big change of the schedule or the reception costs

① 通常情况下，耐心解释，说明情况，并指出潜在的不利影响。

In conventional practice, explain it patiently, state your position, and point out the potential negative effects.

② 如果没有特别的原因，礼貌地拒绝，并说明导游无权不履行合同。

If there is no particular reason, politely decline it and state that the guide is not entitled to make any change in the contract.

③ 如果有特殊原因，向地接社请示汇报。

If there is a special reason, report it to the local travel agency.

（3）双方导游接待计划不一致

inconsistent reception plans of the two sides

① 向地接社汇报并澄清情况，分清责任，征求旅行社的处理意见。

Report it to the local travel agency to clarify the situation, make clear whose responsibility it is and ask for a solution from the agency.

② 如果是地接社的责任，应实事求是地进行解释，赔礼道歉，并执行正确的接待计划。

If it is the local travel agency's fault, give it a factual explanation, offer an apology and carry on the correct reception plan.

③ 如果是组团旅行社的责任，双方友好商量，在双方都能接受的前提下调整行程。

If it is the organizing travel agency's fault, negotiate friendly on adjusting the schedule on the basis of its being accepted by both sides.

（4）特定情形下改变日程或活动计划

change of the itinerary or schedule under particular circumstances

由于不可抗拒因素或突发事件，必须调整原来的计划行程。处理这些案例必须遵守"合理可能"的原则。

Adjustment on the schedule or itinerary must be made due to irresistible force or unexpected incidents. The settlings of these cases are to comply with the "reasonable and possible" principles.

① 旅途中，如遇恶劣天气而不得不改变行程，要耐心地向游客进行解释并调整原定计划。

If the tour is interrupted by bad weather, give explanation patiently to the tourists and adjust the original schedule.

② 关注交通信息，以便在交通阻塞前改变行驶路径。如果不能改变，导游应耐心地向游客进行解释并调整原定计划。

Pay close attention to traffic information in order to be able to make route changes in advance when traffic jams or problems occur. If change fails in such a case, patiently explain it to the tourists and adjust the original schedule.

③ 如果在行程中遇到多数或全部游客感兴趣的活动，如节庆、演出、新景区开放等，在不影响整个行程并确保安全的前提下，征求旅行社的意见后决定是否参与。

During the tour, if the group meet with such events or activities as festival celebrations, shows, openings of new scenic spots, etc. and most or all tourists show great interest in them, and on the promise of no big influence on the entire schedule and safety, ask the receiving travel agency for opinions before making any decision.

④ 遇到航班（班次）取消或延误等交通问题，应当向地接社汇报以便预订下一个航班（班次）。同时，应妥善安排食宿和滞留时间段的游览活动。额外费用由游客支付，要向游客做出合理解释。

When encountering transport problems like flight(train run) cancellations and delays, report it to the receiving travel agency for solution and arrange to book the tickets for the next flight (train run). Meanwhile, arrange for the tourists appropriate board, accommodation and tour in the period. Additional costs should be paid by the tourists, and for that give the tourists a sound explanation.

⑤ 发生了行程延误,还要及时通知下一地点的地接社,以便其做出应变。

Inform the local travel agency of the next stop about the delay so that to give them enough time to take measures for the change.

⑥ 在处理行程延误或错误事故时,要重视游客的意见,如果确认事故是旅行社疏忽所致的,应及时道歉,并向旅行社申请赔偿游客损失。

In dealing with problems of tour delays or errors, listen carefully to tourists' complaints and suggestions. If it is the travel agency's fault, give timely apologies and ask for compensation from the travel agency.

小贴士 Tips

当接待计划有出入时应该如何处理?

当导游(地接导游)手中的接待计划与全导或领队的接待计划有出入时,一般会涉及费用问题。地接导游应该马上报告自己所在的旅行社,查明原因、分清责任。如果是地接社方面的责任,地接导游应该向领队或全程导游实事求是地说明情况并赔礼道歉;如果责任在组团社,地接导游也不能批评对方,而应要求对方做出必要的解释。如果游客要求增添的项目涉及费用,导游应该向旅行社汇报,按规定收取费用并开具发票。一般情况下,地接导游应该采纳、尊重领队或全程导游的意见,同时向自己的旅行社汇报,经旅行社同意后再安排。

课堂实训 In-class Practice

实训项目1　Task 1

情景对话：游客要求改变行程

Dialogue：The Tourists Ask to Change the Itinerary

实训要求：旅游团游客打算在上海购物,要求把上海的行程增加一天,领队金皮尔先生在酒店大堂与导游龚先生商量日程。

Directions：The tourists want to stay in Shanghai for one more day so as to do some shopping. Mr. Ginpil, the tour leader discusses the itinerary with Mr. Gong, the local guide, at the lobby.

示例　Model

（G：local guide, Mr. Gong　L：tour leader, Mr. Ginpil）

L：Mr. Gong, many tourists in the group want to stay one more day in Shanghai for shopping. Is that all right?

G：Oh, I must consult our travel service first before I give you a reply.

（Mr. Gong leaves. After a while, Mr. Gong comes back.）

L：Mr. Gong, sit down, please. What is the reply of your travel service?

G：I am terribly sorry. As the travel service has confirmed hotel and restaurant reservations, it is impossible to make any changes now. I am afraid that we have to go on with our trip according to the itinerary.

L：I can understand. Thanks anyway, Mr. Gong.

实训项目2　Task 2

情景对话：旅游团推迟抵达

Dialogue：The Group Arrival Delays

实训要求：由于旅游团推迟一天到达,要缩短在南京的日程,导游王云与领队金皮尔商量。

Directions：The group arrives one day late. Therefore, the group has to shorten its tour in Nanjing. Miss Wang Yun discusses the new tour plan with Mr. Ginpil.

示例　Model

（G：local guide, Miss Wang Yun　L：tour leader, Mr. Ginpil）

G：Mr. Ginpil, since you arrived a day late, I am afraid that we have to make some changes in the itinerary.

L：Yes. How about shortening the tour in Nanjing? We hope that we can go round Nanjing as much as we can in a day.

G：Ok, I will try my best. (After several minutes) Here is our new itinerary. On the day, we will visit two nearby scenic spots in the morning, another two in the afternoon and have a boat trip on the Qinhuai River in the evening. On the third day we will leave for Shanghai. What do you think of it?

L：It sounds good. We will take this itinerary.

（曾元胜：《中英文导游实训教程》,对外经济贸易大学出版社,2011 年。）

课后实训　After-class Practice

实训项目　Task

情景对话：旅游团被迫提前离开

Dialogue：The Group Has to Leave Earlier than Scheduled

实训要求：假设台风将过境南京,在南京的行程得缩减一天,导游王云与领队金皮尔商量日程。

Directions：Suppose there will be a strong typhoon attacking Nanjing. Therefore, the group has to shorten the tour in Nanjing by one day. Miss Wang Yun discusses the new tour plan with Mr. Ginpil.

示例　Model

（G：local guide, Miss Wang Yun　L：tour leader, Mr. Ginpil）

G：I am terribly sorry, Mr. Ginpil. I am afraid we have to cancel the itinerary of the second day in Nanjing.

L：Why?

G：I've just got a warning notice from the weather observatory and our travel service that there will be a strong typhoon attacking Nanjing on the second day of our planned tour there. Transport systems will stop or be severely affected and all the scenic spots will close.

L：I am really sorry for that. We have no choices but to adjust our itinerary.

G：I suggest canceling the visit to Nanjing Museum, and in the Confucius Temple, you can also know about the culture and folklore of Nanjing, especially those in the Yangtze River Delta.

L：That's a good make-up! I will explain that to the group.

G：Thanks. In order to thank you for your understanding, we will arrange some indoor activities and more local special dishes at supper that day.

L: Thank you very much indeed.

（曾元胜：《中英文导游实训教程》，对外经济贸易大学出版社，2011 年。）

小贴士 Tips

客观原因需要变更计划和日程的处理

旅游过程中，因客观原因，如天气、自然灾害、交通问题等，需要变更旅游团的旅游计划、路线和活动日程时，一般会出现三种情况：

1. 缩短或取消在一地的浏览时间；

2. 延长在一地的游览时间；

3. 在一地的游览时间不变，但被迫取消某一活动，由另一活动代替。

语言储备 Words and Expressions

1. 专业术语 Special Terms

preliminary itinerary	初步行程，初步日程
time distribution	时间分配
flight/train number	航班号/车次
transportation vehicle	交通工具
entrance ticket	门票
tour activity	旅游活动
specific schedules	具体计划
extra cost	额外费用
reception standard	接待标准
self-paying item	自费项目
festival activity	节庆活动
tentative plan	初步计划
the original schedule	原定计划
board and lodging	食宿

2. 实用句型 Useful Sentences

(1) This is the preliminary itinerary I've made. Would you please go over the details?

这是我制订的初步行程,请您看一下细节吧?

(2) I've made this tentative schedule, please have a check.

我草拟了个行程,请您核实。

(3) Have you got anything special in mind that you would like to see?

你们有什么特别想去看的吗?

(4) Are there any special places you are interested in?

有什么地方是你们特别感兴趣的吗?

(5) We have a number of places that are worth visiting.

有许多地方值得参观。

(6) The Xuanwu Lake may be another good choice.

玄武湖也许是另外一个好去处。

(7) Wouldn't it be better to reduce the shopping time to just one hour?

把购物时间减少到仅一小时不是更好吗?

(8) We can shorten lunch time to have more time at the spot.

我们可以缩短午餐时间以便在景点多待一会儿。

(9) I think we'd better make it 10:30, in case there are too many tourists at the spot.

我觉得,我们最好还是定在 10 点半,以免到时景点的人太多。

(10) We will have to cancel the other destination we have planned.

我们将不得不取消原定的另外一个目的地(景点)。

知识链接 Related Knowledge

导游可采取的一般应变措施

1. 制订应变计划并报告旅行社

相关人员要认真分析形势,对问题的性质、严重性和后果做出正确判断;分析游客因情况变化可能出现的心理状态和情绪;迅速就以上情况制订出应变计划并报告旅行社。

2. 做好游客的工作

地接导游、全程导游要就有关问题进行协商,取得一致意见后,找准时机向领队及团中有影响力的游客实事求是地说明困难，诚恳地道歉，以求得原谅，并向他们解释清楚应变计划安排，争取他们的认可和支持，最后分头做游客的工作。

3. 适当给予物质补偿

经旅行社同意，必要时可采取加菜加酒、赠送小纪念品等物质补偿的方法，或者由旅行社出面向游客表达歉意。

4. 延长在一地的游览时间

旅游团因故提前抵达或推迟离开，都会导致一地的游览时间的延长，地接导游应采取的相应措施如下：

（1）与旅行社有关部门联系，重新落实该团用餐、用房、用车的安排。

（2）调整活动日程，酌情增加游览景点，适当延长在主要景点的游览时间，晚上安排文体活动，使活动内容尽可能充实。

（3）如果推迟离开本地要及时通知下一地点导游，也可提醒旅行社与下一地点导游联系。

5. 缩短在一地的游览时间

旅游团因故提前离开或推迟抵达，都会导致一地的游览时间的缩短，地接导游应积极地做好以下工作：

（1）抓紧时间，尽量顺利完成原定的参观游览计划。若确有困难，应有应变计划，但要突出本地最有代表性、最具特色的旅游景点，力求旅游者对本地的旅游景观有基本了解。

（2）如果要提前离开，要及时通知下一地点导游，也可提醒旅行社有关部门与下一地点导游联系。

（3）报告旅行社领导及有关部门，与饭店车队联系，及时办理退餐、退房、退车等事宜。

6. 旅游计划被迫做较大调整

减少半天及以上或取消一地的游览时间，全程导游应报告组团社，由组团社做出决定，并通知有关地方接待旅行社。

（王延君：《模拟导游实务》，北京大学出版社，2012 年。）

模块四　住宿餐饮
Module 4　Accommodation and Catering Service

任务描述 Task Description

　　酒店、饭店是提供安全、舒适的休息或睡眠空间和饮食的场所,主要为游客提供住宿、餐饮、康乐、购物、商务、会议等服务。导游应协助酒店为客人办理入住手续、分配房间,并安排就餐等。

Hotels and restaurants provide accommodations and meals for guests, and also provide healthcare, recreation, hotel shopping, business and meeting services, etc. Tour guides are expected to offer check-in service, assign rooms and arrange meals for tourists.

任务目标 Learning Objectives

　　1. 了解旅游住宿、餐饮服务的具体内容和要求,熟知游客在住宿、就餐时可能会遇到的问题及处理方法。

Know well about what accommodation and meal service is, what problems tourists will have in this aspect and how to solve the problems.

　　2. 熟悉酒店办理入住、分配房间和安排就餐的程序和注意事项。

Be familiar with the procedures of hotel check-in, rooms assignment and meal arrangements, and other matters needing attention.

　　3. 具备处理游客住宿、餐饮等方面问题的能力。

Be able to solve tourists' problems in lodging and catering.

工作流程 Working Process

1. 认真阅读旅游接待计划书和相关材料,详细了解旅游团的食宿服务项目要求。

Read the tour reception plan and related materials carefully, and get the details of the requirements of the accommodation and catering service.

（1）了解入住酒店与目的地的相关信息。

Get enough information about the hotel and the destination.

① 入住酒店的等级、设施和周边情况

grade, facilities and surroundings of the hotel

② 目的地的习俗、饮食文化与禁忌

customs, food culture and taboos of the destination

③ 本地具有代表性的菜点、酒水及其特点、历史渊源

local special dishes and wine and their characteristics, history, etc.

（2）与酒店确认相关事宜。

Confirm related information with the hotel.

① 旅游团食宿的级别标准

standards of accommodation and catering

② 游客入住酒店的天数、住房数、房间类型、入住时间与退房时间、用餐安排

length of stay, numbers and types of rooms, arrival and departure dates, meal arrangements

③ 游客人数、姓名、性别、宗教信仰、分房与用餐要求

number of tourists, names, gender, religious beliefs, room preference, and special request on meals

④ 用餐时间和地点

time and place of meals

⑤ 游客在餐饮和住宿方面的禁忌

tourists' taboos in accommodation and meals

2. 掌握入住酒店的程序、协助办理相关手续,明确下一步的行程（活动）安排,引导游客入住房间。

Master the check-in procedures and relevant requirements, inform the tourists of the follow-up arrangements and guide tourists to their rooms.

（1）办理住店手续。

Check in.

① 抵达酒店后，将游客引导至酒店大堂。

After arriving at the hotel, lead the tourists to the lobby.

② 收齐游客的身份证或护照，准备办理入住手续。

Collect tourists' identification cards or passports for check-in.

③ 与前台人员确定旅游团的名称、房间数量、房型。

Check the name of the tour group, the number of rooms, and the types of rooms.

④ 填写团队入住登记表（表 4-1），领取房间钥匙，准备分发。

Fill in the Hotel Check-in Form for Group (Form 4-1). Get the room keys, ready for handing out.

表 4-1　团体入住登记表

Form 4-1　Hotel Check-in Form for Group

团队编号：

Group Code：

团队名称 NAME OF GROUP	人数 PERSONS	付款单位 CHARGE TO
到达日期 ARRIVAL	离开日期 DEPARTURE	收行李时间 BAGGAGE COLLECTION TIME
押金 DEPOSIT	付款方式 PAYMENT	叫醒时间 WAKE-UP CALL TIME
用餐要求 MEAL REQUIREMENTS		

续表

房间类型、房号及行李 Room Type, Room No. , Luggage			
人数 Persons	房数 Number of Rooms	报账单位 Charge to	签名 Signature
成人 Adults	双人房 Twin		
儿童 Children	双人大床房 Double		
陪同 Guide	加床 Extra		
总计 Total	总计 Total	地陪房号 Room No. of Local Guide	
全陪房号 Room No. of National Guide		领队房号 Room No. of Group Leader	
进店行李 Luggage in	件数 Pieces	行李员签收 Bellman	旅行社签收 Agent
离店行李 Luggage out	件数 Pieces	行李员签收 Bellman	旅行社签收 Agent
备注 Note			

（2）介绍酒店宾客服务指南（表4-2）及相关事项。

Introduce the Service Guide for Hotel Guests (Form 4-2) and the information listed below.

① 酒店的服务设施,如餐厅、商务中心、购物中心、康乐中心等

hotel facilities: restaurants, business center, shopping center, health & recreation center

② 电梯、楼梯的具体位置

locations of elevators, stairs, etc.

③ 酒店房间的设施、收费设施（项目、物品）和使用注意事项

facilities in the rooms, charging items and caution

④ 遇到紧急情况时应采取的措施和求助电话

measures in emergency and phone number for help

表4-2 住店客人服务指南

Form 4-2 Service Guide for Hotel Guests

基本信息 Basic Information	
入住/退房时间 Check-in/Check-out hours	下午2点起办理入住。 Check in from 2:00 p. m. 中午12点前退房。 Check out by 12:00 noon. 24小时接待服务。 Reception is open 24 hours.
客房服务 Guest Room Service	
加床 Extra Beds	3人间提供加床。 Extra beds are available for triple rooms. 每晚每床95美元(包括10%的服务费和税) Extra charge US $95 per night (including 10% service charge and tax)
高速上网 High-speed Internet Access	酒店提供高速上网服务(免费) High-speed Internet connection is available in all the hotel rooms (free of charge).
房间服务 Room Service	房间服务时间: 商务行政套房(24小时) 单人间、标准间(6:00－22:00) 会议中心(6:00－22:00) Room Service is available during the following hours: Business Executive Suite(24 hours) Single/Standard room(6:00 a. m.－10:00 p. m.) Conference Center(6:00 a. m.－10:00 p. m.)
洗衣服务 Laundry Service	提供衣服水洗、干洗、熨烫服务,另收费。 Laundry, dry cleaning and ironing service are available at an extra charge
酒店设施及服务 Hotel Facilities and Services	
停车 Parking	酒店客人免费停车。总停车位:860个。 Free of charge for hotel guests. Total capacity:860.
健身馆 Gymnasium	装备良好的健身房为酒店客人免费开放。 开放时间(6:00－22:00) A well-equipped gym is available to hotel guests at no additional charge from 6:00 a. m. to 10:00 p. m.

续表

机场接送车 Shuttle Bus Service	往返西安咸阳国际机场免费接送服务:24 小时,每 30 分钟一班 Free shuttle bus service is available between the hotel and Xi'an Xianyang International Airport. A bus runs every 30 minutes from 6:00 a. m. to 6:00 p. m.

(3) 宣布当日或次日活动安排。

Announce the arrangements for the day or the next day.

① 告知游客当天的活动安排和集中地点。如当天自由活动,提醒游客外出注意安全。

Tell about the activities for the day, time and place for gathering. Remind tourists of safety matters when they go out.

② 告知游客第二天的叫早时间、早餐时间和地点。

Inform tourists of the next day's wake-up time, breakfast time and place.

③ 宣布次日的行程、集中的时间和地点。

Let the tourists know the following day's arrangement, gathering time and place.

(4) 分发房间钥匙,引领旅游者进房,督促行李员搬运行李到房间。

Hand out the room keys, show tourists to their own rooms and have the bellmen deliver luggage in time.

(5) 巡视房间,协助处理相关问题。

Go around and see if the tourists have any problems. Give them assistance if any.

3. 了解旅游就餐安排的程序、注意事项,引导游客文明就餐,做好相关服务。

Be familiar with the catering arrangement procedures and other matters concerned. See to it that the tourists will enjoy their meals with proper table manners, and give them timely help.

(1) 了解与餐饮相关的信息。

Get the information concerning catering.

① 酒店或餐厅的名称、位置、联系人和联系电话

names of the hotels or restaurants, locations, contact persons and numbers

② 目的地的特色菜、酒水及其特点、历史渊源

special dishes, wine and their characteristics, history, etc.

③ 目的地的习俗、饮食文化与禁忌

characteristics of local customs, food culture and taboos

（2）精心做好就餐安排和服务。

Make meal arrangements properly and be ready to give tourists help.

① 提前落实团队当天的用餐，对午、晚餐的用餐地点、时间、人数、标准、特殊要求逐一核实并确认。

Confirm the meal reservations in advance: times and places of lunch and supper, number of tourists, standards and special requirements of meals.

② 根据团队人数按照旅行社要求合理安排台数。

Arrange the tables with the number of tourists in accordance with the requirements of the travel service.

③ 引导客人进入餐厅入座并清点人数。

Lead tourists to their seats in the restaurant and check the number of tourists.

④ 告知游客自理范围。

Make clear the items on tourists' own expense.

⑤ 用餐时，导游巡视团队用餐情况一到两次，及时解答客人在用餐过程中的问题，并监督餐厅的服务质量，并适时介绍相关特色。

Go around once or twice while dining to answer the tourists' questions and monitor the quality of service, and introduce related specialties.

⑥ 当餐厅上完所有菜后，再次上前征询客人意见，并根据客人的意见在下次订餐时做出相应调整，以满足客人的需要。

Seek for tourists' opinion and suggestions once again after all dishes are served and make adjustments on the next ordering to meet the needs of the tourists.

⑦ 用餐快要结束时，导游告知游客饭后安排。

Announce the after-meal arrangements at the end of the meal.

⑧ 导游需提前结束用餐，以腾出时间与餐厅签结算单。

Finish the meal earlier than others so as to leave time for the bill.

4. 退房，填写"酒店团队费用结算单"（表4-3）。

Check out and fill in *the Group/Company Tour Debit Note*(Form 4-3).

表4-3　酒店团队费用结算单

Form 4-3　Group/Company Tour Debit Note

结算单位： CLIENT					
团队名称： GROUP NAME			陪同姓名： GUIDE NAME		
团队人数： NUMBER OF PERSONS			其中小孩数： NUMBER OF CHILDREN		
入住日期： ARRIVAL DATE			离店日期： DEPARTURE DATE		
项目 DESCRIPTION	结算货币 USD/HKD/RMB	房租 RM RATE	房间数 NO. OF RM	房夜数 RM NIGHTS	小计金额 SUB-TOTAL USD/HKD/RMB
单人房 SINGLE RM					
双人房 TWIN RM					
加床 EXTRA BED					
司陪房 DRIVER/GUIDE RM					
其他 OTHER ITEMS					
房费小计 SUB—TOTAL					
项目 DESCRIPTION	结算货币 USD/HKD/RMB	用餐标准 MEAL STANDARD	人数 PERSONS	餐数 MEALS	小计金额 SUB-TOTAL USD/HKD/RMB
早餐 BREAKFAST					
午餐 LUNCH					
晚餐 SUPPER					
其他 OTHER FOOD					
餐费小计 SUB-TOTAL					

续表

其他 MISCELLANEOUS					
小计 SUB—TOTAL					
收款人全称 NAME OF PAYEE （酒店 HOTEL）			团体费用总额 TOTAL USD/HKD/RMB		
开户银行 BANK OF ACCOUNT					
账号 ACCOUNT NUMBER					

小贴士 Tips

入住酒店礼仪

外出旅行提前预订酒店,这是礼仪,既方便自己,又利于酒店的管理。

1. 预约的礼仪

预订酒店的方式有电话、网络、传真等,但最常用的是电话预订。预订时要告知酒店你的要求、入住的日期、停留的天数、入住的人数、房间的类型、申请住房人的姓名和到达酒店的大概时间,并问清房费。如果比预订时间晚到,尽快联系酒店前台,以免酒店取消预订。

2. 登记入住的礼仪

进入酒店后,首先应该到前台登记。如果携带大量的行李,门童会帮助你,你可以在礼貌地表达谢意后去登记入住。如果前面有正在登记的客人,请安静地排队等候,并与其他客人保持一定的距离。在等候期间,可以提前准备好身份证或者护照。

3. 客房礼仪

客人要保持房间整洁卫生,物品尽量摆放整齐,废弃物要扔进垃圾桶。在洗手间,不要把水溅到地面。床单和牙刷等不必每日都换,牙膏和洗发水用完后再更换。贵重物品可以放在房间内的保险箱或寄存在前台的保险柜。看电视时,应将音量调至适中,并注意看电视的时间，以免影响他人休息。

4. 离店结账礼仪

在离店前打电话告知前台，如果行李很多，可以请前台安排人来帮忙提行李。不要带走酒店的毛巾、睡衣或其他物品。如果不慎损坏了酒店物品，结账时应主动说明并赔偿。结账后，礼貌致谢，道别。

课堂实训　In-class Practice

实训项目1　Task 1

情景对话：确认酒店预订信息

Dialogue：Confirmation of Hotel Reservation

实训要求：来自澳大利亚的18人旅游团，在西安期间将入住赛瑞喜来登酒店。请在旅游团入住前用电话联系酒店前台，确认预订的房间和餐饮，告知对方客人到达的大致时间。

Directions：The Australian tour group of 18 persons will put up in Sheraton Xi'an North City Hotel during their stay in Xi'an. You, the local guide, contact the hotel reception desk by telephone to confirm the room reservation and the meal service. Besides, you should inform them of the approximate arrival time.

示例　Model

（R：hotel receptionist　G：local guide）

R：Sheraton Xi'an North City Hotel. Reception Desk. May I help you？

G：Yes, I'm Zhang Xiaofan from XA ＊＊ Travel Service. I'd like to confirm the reservation for our tour group in your hotel.

R：Oh, I see. May I know the name of your group？

G：Group AU0606 from Australia.

R：For what date or dates？

G：June the 10th.

R：Oh, just a moment, let me have a check. The tour group AU0606 from Australia has reserved 2 single rooms, 3 double rooms, 3 standard rooms and 1 suite for June the 10th. Is there any change?

G：No change at all. Can you tell me how much you will charge for the rooms?

R：For one night, a single room is RMB 550, a standard or double is RMB 580 and a deluxe suite is RMB 860. The above rates include service charge, and a buffet breakfast at Traders Cafe. XA ✳✳ Travel Service is our collaborator and we have very good partnership, so we offer a 30 percent discount. That is 385 for a single, 406 for a standard or double and 602 for a suite.

G：That's great. Could you meet us at the airport?

R：Yes, of course. Our shuttle bus will be waiting for you at the airport. But could you give me the flight number, in case of any delay of the flight?

G：Yes, CA3 ✳✳✳. The flight will be arriving at Xi'an Xianyang International Airport at 11：20. It's a group of 18 tourists, and among them there are 5 vegetarians, please prepare proper food for them.

R：OK. I'll arrange that immediately.

G：That's fine. Thank you.

R：I'm always at your service.

（肖璇：《酒店前台实用英语口语教程》,世界图书出版公司,2011 年。）

实训项目2　Task 2

情景对话：办理团队入住手续

Dialogue：Check-in Service

实训要求：来自澳大利亚的 18 人旅游团,在西安期间将入住赛瑞喜来登酒店。旅游团到达了酒店,请将游客安排在大厅等候,并前往前台办理团队入住手续。

Directions：The Australian tour group of 18 persons will put up in Sheraton Xi'an North City Hotel during their stay in Xi'an. The group arrives at the hotel lobby. You, the local guide, comes to the Reception Desk to check in for the group.

示例　Model

（R：hotel receptionist　G：local guide）

R：Good afternoon, sir. May I help you?

G: Yes, I'd like to check in for my group.

R: Do you have a reservation?

G: Yes. The XA *** Travel Service has booked 2 single rooms, 3 double rooms, 3 standard rooms and 1 suite from for June the 10th. Here is our group number and reservation form. I reconfirmed it before I came.

R: Is there any change in the number of your group tourists?

G: No, 18 tourists.

R: Very good, sir. You have made a reservation for 2 single rooms, 3 double rooms, 3 standard rooms and 1 suite for June the 10th. And the rates include service charge, and a buffet breakfast at Traders Cafe. Is that correct?

G: Yes, exactly. Here are our group's passports.

R: Thank you. I'll make copies; wait a minute, please. Would you please fill in the registration form?

G: OK.

...

R: Sorry to keep you waiting. Here are the room cards. Standard and Double are on the 8th floor; Single and Deluxe Suite on the 12th floor. You can enjoy your breakfast by showing your room card at Traders Cafe, which is on the second floor. Breakfast is from 6: 30 to 10: 00 in the morning. And our bellmen will deliver your luggage to your rooms immediately.

G: Thank you. May I confirm the check-out time?

R: According to the schedule, you will check out at 7: 00 a. m. on the 11th, is it right?

G: Yes, but we would like to change our check-out time to 7: 30 a. m.

R: No problem. Could you please place your luggage outside your room by 7: 00 a. m. on that day? The bellmen will pick them up.

G: OK. Thank you. And the morning call, 6: 30 a. m. for the 11th.

R: I see. Is there anything else I can do for you?

G: No. Thank you.

R: If you need any help, please inform the Front Desk.

G: OK. Thank you.

R: Thank you, enjoy your stay.

实训项目3　Task 3

情景对话：抵达后的第一餐

Dialogue：First Meal after Arriving

实训要求：旅游团入住酒店后，在中国元素餐厅用餐，请陪同游客用好第一餐,简要介绍中国菜,并给游客一些有关菜品选择上的建议。

Directions：The tour group put up at the hotel. They are having their first meal at the Chinese Elements Restaurant. You give them a brief introduction about Chinese food, and help them to make choices.

示例　Model

（G：local guide，Miss Zhang　T1/T2/T3：tourists）

G：Good evening, ladies and gentlemen. You must be tired and hungry after a long trip, so let's have our meal. The restaurant has prepared some local dishes for you, and I hope you'll like them.

T1：(Tasting some) Yes, very delicious, thank you.

G：I'm glad you like the food. The restaurant has prepared 6 local dishes for you, and there are other 6 dishes for you to choose. And here is the menu.

T1：Can you recommend something for us? We've got no idea about Chinese food.

G：You see there're eight famous Chinese cuisines. The dishes we are having are typical Xi'an food. They are tasty, but a little bit salty and oily. And Sichuan cuisine and Hunan cuisine are both spicy.

T1：Spicy? I like spicy dishes.

T2：But it's late in the evening; spicy food is not good for you.

G：What about you, Mrs. Carter?

T3：I'd like to try, but I'm on diet.

G：Well, most of you would like Sichuan cuisine, but as you know, spicy food is not good for health as you'll soon go to sleep. Why not try some tomorrow lunch?

T1：That's a good idea. But, tonight we can't wait to try the eight Chinese cuisines.

G： Besides the local dishes, shall we have some Cantonese food? It's light, and most southerners like it.

T1： Oh, yes. We'd like to try some Cantonese food.

G： How about Soft-boiled Chicken and Steamed Bass? Both of them are popular.

T1： OK, take both of them. And we'd like Lettuce in Oyster Sauce and Mushroom soup.

G： Good, and Cantonese Dim Sum is also very nice. Shrimp Dumplings and Phoenix talons are the most popular ones.

T2： Shrimp Dumplings and Phoenix talons?

G： Yes. Shrimp Dumplings is a delicate steamed dumpling with whole or chopped-up shrimp filling. Phoenix talons are chicken feet, deep fried, boiled, marinated in a black bean sauce and then steamed. That results in a tender, fluffy texture with a strong flavor.

T2： Sounds great. Take both of them.

G： Yes. So we ordered Soft-boiled Chicken, Steamed Bass, Lettuce in Oyster Sauce, Mushroom soup, Shrimp Dumplings and Phoenix talons. I'll tell the waiters at once. And if you have any questions, just let me know. Enjoy your meal.

T1/2： Thanks a lot, Miss Zhang.

小贴士 Tips

餐桌礼仪

1. 餐前穿着：吃饭时穿着得体是欧美人的基本礼仪。去高档餐厅用餐，男士要穿整洁的上衣和皮鞋，女士要穿套装。如果餐厅规定穿正式服装，那么男士必须打领带。

2. 预约：预约时，明确人数和时间，说明对座位的要求，告知宴会的预算。预约一旦确认，应在规定时间内到达。

3. 入座：在西方，右为尊。最得体的入座方式是从左侧入座。不要将手肘放在桌面上，也不可跷足。用餐时，上臂和背部要靠到椅背，腹部和桌子保持一个拳头的距离。

4. 点菜：西餐的上菜顺序是：① 开胃菜(头盘)；② 汤；③ 副菜；④ 主菜；⑤ 蔬菜类菜肴；⑥ 甜品；⑦ 咖啡、茶。没有必要全部都点，开胃菜、主菜加甜品是最恰当的组合。点菜并不是由开胃菜开始点，应先决定主菜，再配上适合主菜的开胃菜或汤。

5. 餐具使用：基本原则是右手持刀或汤匙，左手拿叉。若有两把以上，应由最外面的一把依次向内取用。刀叉的拿法是轻握尾端，食指按在柄上。汤匙则用握笔的方式拿即可。向自己的盘中取食物时，一定要用双手。

6. 用餐：喝汤时，用汤勺从里向外舀，第一匙是"探热"，不要舀太满。吃完汤菜后，将汤匙留在汤盘中，匙把指向自己。吃面包时，把面包用手撕成小片，再缓缓放入口中。吃肉排时，应从左切起。吃鱼时，不要将鱼翻身，吃完一面后用刀叉挑去鱼骨再吃另一面的鱼肉。吃龙虾时，将刀子插入虾壳和虾肉之中，使之剥离，将肉取出后切片享用。

7. 道别致谢：无论何种宴会，离开前都要向女主人当面道别致谢。宴会之后，写信或打电话表示谢意，都是非常得体的。

课后实训　After-class Practice

实训项目1　Task 1

情景对话：入住登记

Dialogue：Check-in

实训要求：一名导游正在为游客办理入住登记手续，根据表格中所给信息，编练有关酒店入住登记的会话。

Directions：A guide is helping his tourists check in at a hotel. Make a conversation between the guide and a tourist according to the instructions below.

Tour guide	Tourist
Ask the tourist to present his passport.	Can't find his passport.
Suggest the tourist check his handbag again.	Still can't find his passport. Get worried.

续表

Tour guide	Tourist
Console the tourist. Advice him to look elsewhere.	Find the passport in the suitcase.
Remind the tourist to be careful with passport.	Express thanks.

示例　Model

（G：local guide　　T：tourist）

G：Now we have arrived at our hotel, please give me your passports and I will help you check in. You can have a rest in the hotel lobby while waiting for me.

T：Oh, God, where is my passport? I can't find it.

G：Relax, is it in your handbag?

T：No, I've checked it for several times. I remember I put it in my handbag last night, but now it isn't there.

G：Did you leave it on our tour bus?

T：No, I left nothing. I'm sure because I checked before getting off.

G：Don't worry. Have you checked your suitcase? Why not open it and have a close look?

T：Ok, let me see. Oh, it's here, in my suitcase. I'm so forgetful. Thanks for your help.

G：My pleasure.

实训项目2　Task 2

情景对话：酒店服务咨询

Dialogue：Hotel Service Inquiry

实训要求：一名导游正在前台询问酒店服务，根据表格中所给信息，编练有关酒店服务的会话。

Directions：A guide is inquiring about the hotel services. Make a conversation between the guide and the receptionist according to the information below.

Items	Details
Check-in time	from 2:00 p.m.
Check-out time	by 12:00 at noon

Items	Details
Internet access	free
International direct call	2 dollars every minute
Room service	call 012
breakfast	from 6:00 to 10:00 a. m.

示例　Model

(R：hotel receptionist　G：local guide)

R：Hello. What can I do for you, sir?

G：Hello. Our group just checked in this afternoon. May I ask some questions?

R：Of course, sir.

G：What is the check-in and check-out time in the hotel?

R：The check-in time usually begins from 2:00 p. m. and guests are expected to check out by 12:00 at noon.

G：Can we use the internet access here?

R：Yes, we offer free internet service to our guests.

G：Thank you. And how can I make an international direct call from my room?

R：First, you need to pay a deposit of 60 dollars at the reception desk. Then you can make the phone call in your room. The rate is 2 dollars per minute.

G：I see. One more thing, how can I order room service?

R：You can just call 012 and tell them what you want, and they'll send what you ordered to your room as soon as possible. We offer 24-hour room service and you can find the menu by the TV set in your room.

G：Thanks. What about breakfast time?

R：From 6:00 a. m. to 10:00 a. m. , sir.

G：Thanks a lot.

R：You are welcome. Enjoy your stay.

(王哲：《旅游英语》，外语教学与研究出版社，2011 年。)

实训项目3　Task 3

情景对话：用餐安排

Dialogue：Meal Arrangements

实训要求：一名导游正在向游客介绍就餐安排,根据表格中所给信息,编练相关会话。

Directions：A guide is introducing meal arrangements to the tourists. Make a conversation between them according to the instructions below.

Tour guide	Tourist
Introduce the place of supper.	Give responses.
Introduce specials in the restaurant.	Show interest in the specials. Say you are allergic to onions.
Promise to tell the cook not to put onions in the dishes.	Express gratitude.

示例 Model

（G：local guide   T：tourist）

G：Ladies and gentlemen, I think you are all hungry after a long journey. And now we'll have supper at the dining hall on the second floor.

T：Very good. We are hungry and we can't wait to try Chinese food.

G：The restaurant has arranged some Chinese special food for you：Pita Bread Soaked in Lamb Soup, Sweet and Sour Mandarin Fish and Steamed Beef Ribs in Black Bean Sauce. I believe you'll like them.

T：Oh, it sounds great. But I am allergic to onion.

G：Don't worry about that. I'll tell the cook not to put onion in your dish.

T：Thank you very much.

G：You are welcome.

语言储备 Words and Expressions

1. 专业术语 Special terms

single room	单人间
double room	双人(床)间
king size bed room	大床间
twin(-bed) room/standard room	两床间/标准间
triple room	三人间
family suite	家庭套房
presidential suite	总统套间

business suite	商务套房
garden view room	园景房
sea view room	海景房
non-smoking room	无烟标准间
handicapped room	残疾人客房
room with kitchen	带厨房客房
floor attendant	楼层服务员
assign rooms	分配房间
morning/wake-up call	叫醒服务,叫早电话
dining hall	餐厅
rooming list	分房名单表
registration form	登记表
Beijing Roast Duck	北京烤鸭
sautéed shredded pork in sweet bean sauce	京酱肉丝
braised spare ribs	酱烧排骨
sautéed pork with mushrooms	珍菌滑炒肉
bamboo shoots and green beans	竹笋青豆
stir-fried diced chicken with walnuts	鸡丁核桃仁
soft-boiled chicken	白切鸡
steamed bass	清蒸鲈鱼
lettuce in oyster sauce	蚝油生菜
mushroom soup	蘑菇汤
shrimp dumplings	虾饺
phoenix talons in black bean sauce	豉汁凤爪
steamed beef ribs in black bean sauce	豉汁蒸排骨
crispy beef filet	酥皮牛柳
quick-fried pork filet slices with sauce	滑溜里脊片
braised pork intestines with mashed garlic	蒜香烩肥肠
sweet and sour mandarin fish	松鼠鳜鱼
pita bread soaked in lamb soup	羊肉泡馍

2. 实用句型　Useful sentences

(1) Have you made a reservation?

　　有预订吗?

（2）We have no record of a reservation in your name.

没有你名下的预订。

（3）Would you please complete this registration form?

请把这份表格填一下。

（4）Could you sign your name here, please?

请在这里签名。

（5）Leave it to me. I'll take care of your baggage.

把您的行李交给我吧。

（6）Car rental service is available in our hotel.

我们酒店有汽车出租服务。

（7）There are safety deposit boxes at the Front Desk.

前台有保险箱供放置贵重物品。

（8）The newsstand has a wide selection of foreign newspapers and magazines.

报亭有许多外国报纸和杂志供阅读。

（9）We will have breakfast at 7：00 a. m. on the second floor of the hotel.

我们早7点在酒店二楼用早餐。

（10）We'll have a buffet lunch with a good variety of options.

中餐我们吃自助餐,有很多菜品供选择。

（11）We'd like to have a full Chinese meal.

我们想吃一顿正宗的中餐。

（12）Here is the menu. What would you like to have?

这是菜单,你们想吃些什么?

（13）Roast duck is the specialty here.

烤鸭是这里的特色菜。

（14）Dongpo meat is one of the most famous dishes in Hangzhou.

东坡肉是杭州最有名的菜肴之一。

（15）I'd like to have some local dishes.

我想吃点本地菜。

（16）How is the dinner (meal)?

吃得怎样?

（17）Is the roast duck all right?

烤鸭怎么样?

（18）Do you like the fish cooked this way?

你喜欢这种烧法的鱼吗?

（19）Let me recommend our special dishes to you.

我来给你们推荐特色菜。

（20）We have a good variety of Chinese food and wines at your choice.

有各种各样的菜肴和酒供大家选择。

知识链接 Related Knowledge

国际五星级酒店分类

国际五星级酒店品牌类别是根据世界各大著名酒店集团的各个子品牌进行分类的。

国际五星级酒店分为：奢华五星级酒店（LUXURY 5 STAR HOTEL）、精品五星级酒店（BOUTIQUE 5 STAR HOTEL）、豪华五星级酒店（DELUXE 5 STAR HOTEL）、普通五星级酒店（5 STAR HOTEL）。

1. 奢华五星级酒店（LUXURY 5 STAR HOTEL）：BVLGARI（宝格丽）、Ritz-Carlton（丽思卡尔顿/丽嘉）、Four Seasons（四季）、Park Hyatt（柏悦）、Peninsula（半岛）、Mandarin Oriental（文华东方）、Waldorf（华尔道夫）、Luxury Collection（至尊精选）、Fairmont（费尔蒙）、Sofitel Legend（索菲特传奇）、Rosewood（瑰丽）。

2. 精品五星级酒店（BOUTIQUE 5 STAR HOTEL）：Aman（安缦）、Banyan Tree（悦榕庄）、Anantara（安纳塔拉）、Rustic Luxury（野奢）、Indigo（英迪格）、Andaz（安达仕）、Sofitel So（索菲特）。

3. 豪华五星级酒店（DELUXE 5 STAR HOTEL）：Conrad（康莱德/港丽）、Kempinski（凯宾斯基）、Langham（朗廷）、Intercontinental（洲际）、JW Marriott（JW 万豪）、Grand Hyatt（君悦）、Regent（丽晶）、Westin（威斯汀）、Le Meridien（艾美）、Gran Melia（美利亚）、Puli（璞丽）、Wyndham Grand Plaza（温德姆至尊豪廷）、Shangri-La（香格里拉）。

4. 标准五星级酒店（STANDARD 5 STAR HOTEL）：Hilton（希尔顿）、Hyatt（海悦）、Crowne Plaza（皇冠假日）、Sheraton（喜来登）、Marriott（万豪）、Pullman（铂尔曼）、Ramada Plaza（华美达广场）、Howard Johnson（豪生）、Grand Mercure（美爵）、Radisson Blu Plaza（丽笙）、Nikko（日航）、Renaissance（万丽）、Langham Place（郎豪）。

模块五 游览服务

Module 5 Sightseeing Service

任务描述 Task Description

参观游览既是旅游活动中最重要的部分,又是导游活动的中心环节。导游的参观游览服务主要包括出发前的准备工作、沿途导游、景点导游讲解和参观返程中的工作。

Sightseeing is the most important activity in travelling and the key part of the guiding service. For the sightseeing service, a tour guide should get well prepared in advance, make on-the-way introductions, give scenic spot explanations, and fulfill job duties en route back to the hotel.

任务目标 Learning Objectives

1. 了解参观游览前的准备工作内容;掌握沿途导游讲解的方法;能熟练并专业化地进行景点导游讲解;熟悉参观返程工作流程;掌握相关的基本词汇和表达。

Get familiar with the preliminary work before going to the scenic spots. Master professional approaches for the on-the-way introductions. Be able to give scenic spot introduction adeptly and expertly. Be familiar with the service on the way back. Grasp the basic vocabulary and expressions concerned.

2. 能够专业化地实施旅游团参观游览服务的各项具体工作程序;能够熟练地运用英文与外国旅游团进行交流,随时随地竭诚为游客服务。

Operate all the specific work procedures during the sightseeing service professionally. Communicate with foreign tour groups in English fluently during sightseeing activities, and be always at their service.

3. 培养良好的服务意识、耐心细致的工作作风、文明有礼的工作习惯。

Develop good service consciousness, cultivate patient and considerate work habits, and always be in good manners at work.

工作流程 Working Process

1. 准备工作

Preliminary Work

（1）做好物质准备。出发前准备好旅行社社旗、导游证、话筒（扩音设备）、中英文当地旅游地图册和必要的票证，至少提前 10 分钟到达集合地点，并督促司机做好各项准备工作。

Get everything prepared before going to the tourist attractions, including the travel agency's flag, tour guide certificate, microphone (or loud speaker), local maps in both Chinese and English, and tickets if necessary. Arrive at the gathering place at least 10 minutes ahead of time, and remind the driver to be well prepared.

（2）核实、清点人数。及时与领队、全程导游接洽，核对旅行团的国别（或地区）、人数、客源地组团社的名称、领队和全导的姓名。如果有游客未及时赶到，应向领队或全程导游问明原因，设法让其尽快归队；如果有游客留在酒店或不随团活动，应问清原因并进行妥善安排，必要时报告酒店有关部门。

Contact the tour leader or the national guide. Check and verify the country (or region) the group is from, the number and the names of the tourists, and the names of the domestic tour operator, the tour leader and the national guide. If there are tourists who fail to arrive on time, ask the tour leader or the national guide for reasons and contact the tourists at once. If there are tourists who choose to stay at the hotel or do not want to go with the group, inquire about their reasons and make necessary arrangements, and tell the hotel about the situation if necessary.

（3）提醒注意事项。向旅行团预报天气和游览路线等情况，提醒游客带好随身物品、外套、雨伞、太阳镜、防晒霜等，并告知其游览的注意事项等。

Tell the tour group about the local weather forecast for the day and the itinerary in advance. Remind them to take their personal belongings and things like coat, umbrella, sun glasses and sun cream, and to remember some dos and don'ts for sightseeing, etc.

（4）准点集合登车。在早餐前再次提醒游客集合的时间和地点。游客到齐后,清点人数并请游客上车。应在车门一侧恭候,礼貌得体地招呼游客登车,协助老弱者上车。开车前,务必再次清点人数。

Remind the tour group of their gathering time and place once more before breakfast. Check the number of the tourists before and after they get on the coach. Stand by the coach door to assist the tourists to get on, and give special care to the old and the weak. Make sure that all the tourists are seated before departure.

2. 沿途介绍

On-the-way Introduction

（1）介绍当天的活动安排。在车上向游客表示欢迎,介绍参加接待的司机等人员,并介绍城市概况和在当地游览的活动安排,同时提醒游客旅行的注意事项,最后表达为大家热情服务、确保大家满意的意愿和态度。

Extend your warm welcome to the tour group, introduce your colleagues including the driver, and briefly describe the city and the tour schedule on the way. Remind the tourists of what they should pay attention to, and express your best wishes for a pleasant trip.

（2）前往景点途中进行沿途风光介绍,将沿途所见具有代表性的景物向游客做简要介绍,并回答游客的提问。

On the way to the tourist attractions, introduce some representative scenic spots that the group pass by and answer tourists' questions if any.

（3）抵达景点前应向游客简要介绍该景点,让大家事先了解相关信息,激发其游览兴趣。

Before arriving at the destination, give a brief introduction so as to give the tourists a general picture of what they will visit and, meanwhile, to arouse their interest.

（4）如果途中时间较长,可以在车内开展一些娱乐活动,让游客们参与其中,以消除大家舟车劳顿,活跃旅途气氛。

If it is a long way to cover, arrange some appropriate on-bus games to keep tourists in high spirits and make them feel less bored or tired.

3. 景点导游

Scenic Spot Guiding Service

（1）抵达景点时,在下车前交代清楚并提醒游客记住旅游大巴的标志、车号、颜色、停车地点和开车时间。进入景点后,在景点示意图前讲明游览路线、所需时间、集合时间和地点等,并讲明参观游览过程中的有关注意事项。

On arriving at the scenic spot, inform tourists of the coach mark, number and color, the parking lot and expected time of departure. With the help of the tour sketch map at the entrance, tell the tourists about the tour route, expected visiting time, gathering time and location. Inform the tourists of matters that need attention during their visit at the scenic spot.

（2）讲解内容应繁简适度,包括景点的历史背景、文化特色、地位和价值等。游览过程中应手举导游旗走在旅游队伍前面,做到边引路边讲解,并面带微笑。选择最佳的讲解位置,一般离游客1米左右即可,或请游客围在自己身旁讲解,并特别关照老弱旅游者。

Give a comprehensive and clear scenic spot explanation or introduction, which often includes its historical background, cultural characteristics, status and value. Hold the guide flag in hand, lead the tour group with a smile and make introductions while moving on. When stopping to make an introduction before a spot, select a proper place either with the tourists standing about one meter away from you or around you. Take special care of the old and the weak.

（3）景点导游中,留意游客们的动向,要自始至终与其一起活动。要和全程导游、领队密切配合并随时清点人数,防止意外事件的发生。

Pay close attention to the tourists' whereabouts during the tour, and be always at their service. Meanwhile, closely cooperate with the national guide and the tour leader. Check the number of the tourists whenever necessary, in case of any possible mishap or accident.

4. 返程工作
Job Duties en Route Back

（1）返程时,再次清点人数后上车。回顾当天参观游览的内容,必要时做补充讲解,并回答游客们的提问。

Check the number of the tourists again after everybody gets on the coach. On the way back, review the sightseeing activities of the day, give supplementary explanation of the visited places if necessary and of course, answer questions from the tourists.

（2）返程路途中,如果游客不太累,可组织一些娱乐活动调节气氛,但要适可而止。

Organize some on-bus games if the tourists are not tired in order to create a cheerful atmosphere.

（3）返回酒店下车前，宣布次日的活动安排、出发时间和集合地点等，同时提醒游客带好随身物品。先下车，然后照顾游客依次下车，再与他们告别。

Before reaching the hotel, inform tourists of the next day's arrangement, gathering and departure time, etc. Remind them to take all their belongings when getting off the coach. Stand by the coach door to help the tourists get off one by one and say goodbye to them genially.

小贴士 Tips

导游仪表礼仪

一、男导游

1. 短发，保持头发清洁、整齐，发型不要太新潮。

2. 精神饱满，面带微笑。

3. 每天刮胡须，不留指甲，饭后洁牙。

4. 着装整洁、自然、便于活动，衣服颜色控制在三种以内。

二、女导游

1. 发型文雅、庄重，梳理整齐，长发要用发卡夹好。

2. 化淡妆，面带微笑。

3. 着装整洁、大方、得体，裙子长度适宜，肤色丝袜，衣服颜色控制在三种以内。

4. 指甲不宜过长，保持清洁；若涂指甲油，须为自然色。

5. 戴首饰要适度。

课堂实训　In-class Practice

实训项目 1　Task 1

情景对话：接洽领队

Dialogue：Meet the Tour Leader

实训要求：来自澳大利亚的 18 人旅游团 AU0606 将如期到达南京。假设你是

南京 ** 旅行社的王小姐,受委派成为该团在南京期间的导游。在酒店大堂等待游客集合时,你事先与领队金皮尔先生接洽,确认行程安排和注意事项。

Directions: The tour group AU0606 of 18 tourists from Australia arrived at Nanjing on schedule. Suppose you are Miss Wang from Nanjing ** Travel Service, and will be the local guide for the group. You meet the tour leader Mr. Ginpil in advance so as to confirm the itinerary and discuss some issues with him and meanwhile wait for the tour group in the hotel lobby.

示例　**Model**

(G: local guide, Miss Wang　　L: tour leader, Mr. Ginpil)

G: Good morning, Mr. Ginpil.

L: Good morning, Miss Wang.

G: Did you sleep well last night?

L: Very well, thank you, and you?

G: Fine, thanks. Mr. Ginpil, here is our tour schedule.

L: OK, let me have a look. Ah, we'll visit Dr. Sun Yat-sen's Mausoleum and the Ming Tomb today. Are there any dos and don'ts for this visit?

G: Yes. According to the local beliefs, the sacred statues in the Ming Tomb should not be photographed, and don't step on the threshold or make any noise when entering the Memorial hall or temple. I'll tell the tourists when they gather together.

L: All right. Anything else?

G: Also, I think we'd better remind everyone to take their umbrellas or raincoats with them because there is rain according to the weather forecast.

L: Thank you. I'll tell everybody right away.

G: Good. There are 18 tourists in this tour group, including 3 seniors, 5 vegetarians and 2 kids. Is that right?

L: Exactly.

G: So I have to pay more attention to them during the trip. But, are they all clear of our gathering time and place?

L: Yes, I told them last night.

G: Well, we will be ready to leave at 8 o'clock, OK?

L: OK, see you later.

G：See you.

（李燕：《旅游英语》，清华大学出版社，2009 年。）

实训项目2   Task 2

情景对话：介绍当天行程安排

Dialogue：Introduce the Tour Arrangement for the Day

实训要求：来自澳大利亚的旅游团 AU0606 已经从酒店出发，正前往南京的旅游目的地。在途中，请以地接导游王小姐的身份向游客介绍此次的行程安排，并回答游客提出的相关问题。

Directions：The tour group AU0606 from Australia has set off for their sightseeing destinations in Nanjing. On the way, you, the local guide Miss Wang, give a brief introduction about the tour arrangement during their stay in Nanjing, and answer questions from the tourists.

示例   Model

（G：local guide   T：tourist）

G：Good morning, ladies and gentlemen. Now I'd like to introduce the schedule for your stay here in Nanjing. Today, we will first go to Dr. Sun Yatsen's Mausoleum, which is well-known throughout the country, and visit the Ming Tomb, Linggu Temple and Hongshan Forest Zoo. Tomorrow, we'll first visit Nanjing Yangtze River Bridge and the Presidential Palace. In the afternoon, we'll go to the Confucius Temple, and Qinhuai Scenic Zone. They are very popular and beautiful tourist attractions, and we'll have lunch and supper in the special local restaurants there to taste some local delicacy. And in the evening, we'll enjoy the beautiful scenes along the Qinhuai River. So, any questions?

T：Yeah, can you tell me something about the Ming Tomb?

G：The Ming Tomb was first built in 1381, which has a long history of more than 600 years. It is one of the key national cultural relics, protected under the approval of the State Council in 1961. In 2003, it was enlisted in the World Cultural Heritage Directory by UNESCO.

T：Fantastic! Well, can we stop somewhere to buy local handicrafts and souvenirs?

G：Yes, of course. Tomorrow we'll visit the Confucius Temple, and it is also a big shopping area, where you can buy handicrafts and other local souvenirs.

T：Thank you very much.

G：You are welcome.

（李燕：《旅游英语》，清华大学出版社，2009 年。）

实训项目 3　Task 3

模拟讲解：中山陵

Speech：Dr. Sun Yat-sen's Mausoleum

实训要求：经过半小时的车程，澳大利亚旅游团 AU0606 到达了中山陵景区。请以地接导游王小姐的身份为旅游团提供中山陵景区的导游讲解，使用英文向游客介绍中山陵，并提供专业的导游服务。

Directions：After half an hour's drive, the tour group AU0606 from Australia arrive at their destination, Dr. Sun Yat-sen's Mausoleum. You, the local guide Miss Wang, please give a scenic spot introduction while the tourists are visiting. You are required to do it in English, and provide professional guiding service as well.

示例　Model

Dr. Sun Yatsen's Mausoleum

Ladies and gentlemen, Dr. Sun Yat-sen's Mausoleum is the best known historic and cultural tourist attraction in Nanjing. It sits on the southern slope of the Purple Mountain in the eastern suburb of the city and covers an area of eighty thousand square meters. The construction of Dr. Sun Yat-sen's Mausoleum began in the spring of 1926, and it took 3 years and 1.5 million silver dollars to finish.

Dr. Sun Yat-sen, also named Sun Wen or Sun Zhongshan, was the forerunner of the Chinese democratic revolution. He was born in a peasant family in Guangdong Province on October 12, 1866 (the late Qing Dynasty). Sponsored by his elder brother, he was first educated in Hawaii. Upon his return, he dreamed to save the nation by practicing medicine when he was only 21 years old. However, the reality made him turn to politics in 1893. From then on, he kept on petitioning to the Qing government for reforms but was never responded. At great disappointment, he left for the USA, Europe and Japan, trying to win the sympathy and support from overseas Chinese. With the funds raised, he organized "Revive China League"—the first bourgeois organization in China, with a clear-cut aim of "Expel Tartars, Restore China, Establish Republic and Equalized Land". Also, he put forth the great three democratic principles, named "Nationalism, Democracy and People's Livelihood", as his political goal.

The most important event was the 1911 Revolution in Wuhan led by Dr. Sun, which drove the last Qing emperor out of the Forbidden City in Beijing, marking the end of the dynastic system lasting for 2400 years in China. On January 1,1912, it was in Nanjing that the first republic in Chinese history was founded and Dr. Sun Yat-sen inaugurated his presidency.

Unfortunately, the new republic was threatened by the powerful warlords in the north. China went into chaotic civil wars at that time. Despite his poor health, Dr. Sun Yat-sen was dedicated to his political career, and officially acknowledged the cooperation between the Nationalist Party and the Communist Party in 1924. On March 12, 1925, Dr. Sun Yat-sen passed away in Beijing.

Dr. Sun Yat-sen's Mausoleum is designed in the shape of a liberty bell for the purpose of reminding people never to get self-contented. The whole construction, from the gateway to the main entrance, tablet pavilion, memorial hall to the tomb vault, lies on the north-to-south axis with 392 steps and 10 platforms in between. All the buildings are constructed with natural granite and marble, with blue glazed tile roofs.

Now, we are approaching to the gateway. This 12-meter high building has three arches, with Dr. Sun Yat-sen's handwriting "Fraternity" carved high on its front. Further from the Fraternity Archway, there is a road leading to the mausoleum. The road is 480 meters long and dozens of meters wide, lined with pine, gingko and maple trees, which shows not only a traditional style of grandness and solemnity, but also Dr. Sun Yat-sen's revolutionary spirit and lofty quality.

Well, we are coming near the top platform. Look, there are two big copper "dings". At the bottom of the left one, there are two holes because of the Japanese shootings in late 1937 when the Japanese army attacked Nanjing. Today, although we have a peaceful life, the two holes always remind our Chinese people not to forget the national humiliation at that time. Here, we can have a bird-view of what it is in the distance.

Now, we are in front of the Memorial Hall and the coffin chamber. These are the most basic guiding principles of Dr. Sun Yat-sen's revolutionary activities. Above "Democracy", there is a horizontal inscription board with Sun's handwriting as well as his motto "The World Belongs to the People" on it. Please follow me into the Memorial Hall. The floor is covered with white and black marble from Yunnan Province. In the center, you can see Dr. Sun Yat-sen's statue mounted on a pedestal, which was built with the Italian white marble by a Polish sculptor. The surrounding walls are inscribed with the national constitution written by Dr. Sun Yat-sen. Beyond the memorial hall is the tomb vault. Standing by the pool, if you look down, you will bow to see Dr. Sun Yat-sen's reclining marble statue with his body buried 5 meters underneath. If you look up, you will find the emblem of the Nationalist Party on the ceiling. The whole architectural style is a blend of the Eastern and the Western, representing well blended doctrines of Dr. Sun Yat-sen.

Ladies and gentlemen, Dr. Sun Yat-sen struggled for a better China throughout his life. He overthrew the monarch feudalist system which lasted for more than 2000 years in China. The great feat Mr. Sun achieved has gained great respect and praise both at home and abroad. Standing on this top platform of the mountain, you will not only feel entirely relieved since you've covered 392 steps, but also enjoy a bird's-eye view of the beautiful Nanjing city. Nowadays, as one of the "Top Forty Tourist Resorts in China", Dr. Sun Yat-sen's Mausoleum attracts numerous Chinese and international tourists every year. OK, thank you for your attention and cooperation!

（江苏省旅游局：《走遍江苏(英文版)》，中国林业出版社，2000 年。）

实训项目4 Task 4

模拟讲解：致欢送辞

Speech：Make a Farewell Speech

实训要求：澳大利亚旅游团 AU0606 正在返回酒店的途中。请以地接导游的身份向旅游团致欢送辞，简要回顾当天的活动并告知游客第二天的行程安排。

Directions：The tour group AU0606 from Australia is on their way back to the hotel. As the local guide, you deliver a farewell speech to the tourists before they get off the coach, briefly reviewing the trip for the day and explaining the travel schedule for the next day.

示例　Model

Farewell Speech

Ladies and gentlemen, how time flies! It's a pity that your trip in Nanjing is drawing to a close. Then, please allow me to take this opportunity to say goodbye to you here.

I'd like to tell you that it is a great pleasure for me to be your tour guide in the past two days. It's nice to have known you, and spent plenty of time together with you. For sightseeing, we have visited Dr. Sun Yat-sen's Mausoleum, the Ming Tomb, Linggu Temple, Hongshan Forest Zoo, Nanjing Yangtze River Bridge, the Presidential Palace, Qinhuai Scenic Zone, and the Confucius Temple, where we've learned more about this beautiful city.

We are now on the way back to the hotel and will arrive there in half an hour. Since I won't accompany you to the hotel, there are a few things I'd like to mention. As we are about to leave for Shanghai by CRH at 7:20 tomorrow morning, we need to get up earlier than usual. I have already arranged a 5:30 morning call, and the time for breakfast is between 6:00 and 6:30. We should meet in the lobby at 6:45. Please remember to pack up all your belongings before that. The travel from Nanjing to Shanghai will take us nearly 2 hours. Hope you have a good sleep tonight!

We highly appreciate all the cooperation and support you've given in the past two days. You are so time-keeping and attentive, which made my job easier and happier. We have become good friends. There is an old Chinese saying "A bosom friend afar brings a distant land near". Wish all of you would remember this trip! If there is anything we could do for you, please don't hesitate to contact us.

Once more, thank you for your cooperation and support. Goodbye!

（李燕:《旅游英语》, 清华大学出版社, 2009 年。）

小贴士 Tips

导游词的创作

1. 创作技巧

（1）景点主题要正确、明确。

（2）写作内容要新颖、独特。

（3）景点提示要有文化内涵。

2. 基本要求

（1）准确。准确性差表现在：

① 对史实掌握不准，以讹传讹，误导旅游者；

② 片面追求导游趣味，以野史代替正史，内容低俗，丧失严肃性；

③ 语言表达不准，语法错误较多，用词不够精当，容易引起误解。

（2）鲜明。为达到鲜明效果，可采取排比、对比、递进和反复等方法。

（3）具体。主要内容要具体，次要内容需精炼。

（4）生动。要素包括：绘声绘色、细致刻画、生动形象、幽默诙谐。

3. 导游词＝正确和明确的主题思想＋景点深刻的内涵＋贯穿全篇统一的相关知识＋优美生动和风趣幽默的言辞。

（《导游服务技能》编写组：《导游服务技能》，中国旅游出版社，2014 年。）

课后实训 After-class Practice

实训项目 1 Task 1

情景对话：沿途介绍服务——城市简介

Dialogue：On-the-way Introduction Service—City Introduction

实训步骤 Steps

第一步：学生分组扮演地接导游和游客。

Step 1：Divide the class into groups to play the roles of the local guide and tourists.

第二步：准备导游旗、麦克风及旅游行程安排材料和游客相应信息。

Step 2：Prepare a guide flag, a microphone, a tour itinerary and tourist information.

第三步：完成地接导游与游客在途中的对话，提供简要的城市介绍，回答游客提出的问题。

Step 3：Make a dialogue between the local guide and a tourist. Provide on-the-way introduction service about the city to be visited. Answer questions from tourists.

示例　Model

（G：local guide　T：tourist）

G：Good morning, ladies and gentlemen. Welcome to the capital city of Jiangsu Province—Nanjing. I'm very honored to be your local guide and show you around this beautiful city during your stay here. Now, may I introduce my colleague to you? This is Mr. Ma Le, our driver, who has a driving experience of more than 20 years. My name is Wang Yun from Nanjing ** Travel Service. My job is to give you good service, care for your welfare, answer your questions and of course, give you scenic spot explanation while you are visiting. My cell phone number is 150 ** 442435, and our driver's is 138 ** 463782. Our bus is white and its number is 苏 A 90 *** , please remember it. Perhaps, it's the first time for most of you to visit Nanjing, so I'd like to give you a brief introduction about this city. As the capital city of Jiangsu Province, Nanjing is located in the lower reaches of the Yangtze River, southwest of the province, with a population of more than 8.2 million in 2014. Owing to its superior location and splendid history, the city has remained to be the political, economic and cultural center in the Yangtze Delta Region. Once being called the southern capital of China, Nanjing is one of the most famous historic and cultural cities named by the State Council. Now, it enjoys a worldwide reputation. In the city, there are a lot of places of interests and scenic spots worth visiting, such as Dr. Sun Yatsen's Mausoleum, the Ming Tomb, Qinhuai scenic zone, the Confucius Temple and so on. Thus, wish all of you have a pleasant journey!

T：Excuse me, Miss Wang. When will we get to Dr. Sun Yat-sen's Mausoleum?

G：Well, it is only a 15 minute drive there.

T：Could you tell me what it is famous for?

G：It is famous for its historic stories and beautiful scenery. I believe you would like it.

T：Great! I'm interested in Chinese history and culture, and I've heard a little about Dr. Sun Yat-sen's Mausoleum in Nanjing.

G：Good. That is also why most foreign tourists prefer this place. Hope you enjoy your trip!

T：Thank you very much.

G：You are welcome.

实训项目2　Task 2

模拟讲解：明孝陵景区

Speech：The Ming Tomb

实训步骤　Steps

第一步：学生分组扮演地接导游和游客。

Step 1：Divide the class into groups to play the roles of the local guide and tourists.

第二步：准备导游旗、麦克风以及旅游行程安排材料；做好相关景点讲解的准备。

Step 2：Prepare a guide flag, a microphone and a tour itinerary; Make a good preparation for the scenic spot introduction.

第三步：提供明孝陵景点导游讲解服务。

Step 3：Make scenic spot introduction of the Ming Tomb.

示例　Model

The Ming Tomb

Ladies and gentlemen, the Ming Tomb is the mausoleum of Zhu Yuanzhang, the founding emperor of the Ming Dynasty about 600 years ago. The construction of the mausoleum started in 1381, and was completed in 1413 when the Tablet of Great Merits of the Ming Tomb for the Great Ming Dynasty was erected.

Zhu Yuanzhang was born in a poor peasant family in Fengyang County of Anhui Province in 1328. He lost his parents in his childhood and became a monk at the Huangjue Temple. At the age of 25, he joined the Hongjin Army, a force against the government. Soon he became the head of the Army, and took over Nanjing in 1356. Only in 2 years, he conquered the rest parts of China, and established his empire and made Nanjing the capital with the name of Ming for his dynasty. Zhu Yuanzhang began to have his tomb built when his wife died. The empress was buried in the tomb in 1383, and Emperor Zhu Yuanzhang was buried here in 1398 after his death.

Now, please follow my steps. The mausoleum consists of two main sections. The front section starts from the Gateway of Dismounting Horses at the Filial Guard to the Lingxing Gate at the end of the Sacred Way. Serving as the tomb avenue, this part is 1800 meters long. The Gateway of Dismounting Horses is engraved with 6 Chinese characters for warning worships, meaning *All the officials must dismount from their horses back here*. It shows the absolute dignity of Emperor Zhu Yuanzhang at that time.

Go 700 meters northwest from the gateway, and we can see a three-arched gate. It is known as the Grand Golden Gate, which is the front gate of the mausoleum, connecting the red enclosure walls.

Let's go through the Grand Golden Gate. Now you see the roofless pavilion. It is called the Square City. In the middle of the pavilion there stands a huge stone tablet, which is 8.78 metres high with 2,746 characters carved on it. This is the Tablet of Great Merits of the Ming Tomb for the Great Ming Dynasty. The characters were written by Zhu Di, the third emperor of the Ming Dynasty.

Now we are on the Sacred Way. The Sacred Way is divided into two sections. As you can see, the front section is flanked by 12 pairs of stone animals in 6 kinds: each kind of the animals has 2 pairs, one standing and the other kneeling. The animals are arranged in a proper order: lions, Xiezhi, camels, elephants, unicorns and horses.

At the end of the Sacred Way, there is the Lingxing Gate, also called the Dragon & Phoenix Gate. About 270 meters away from the gate is the stone bridge spanning over a stream, which is named the Imperial Moat Bridge. The bridge once had 5 arches, but was renovated into 3 arches later in the Qing Dynasty.

About 200 meters north of the bridge is the front gate of the tomb. At the right of the gate there is a tablet stone, which is inscribed with "The Special Notice" in 6 foreign languages to call for attention to protect the tomb. The tablet was established by the Qing government.

Inside the gate is a tablet pavilion, which is the entrance hall of the tomb. In this pavilion, there's a tablet inscribed with the Stele of "Administrating the country as prosperous as the Tang and Song Dynasties". The inscription was written by Kangxi, an emperor of the Qing Dynasty, when he was paying his homage to the entombed emperor during his third inspection tour to the area in 1699.

Going out of the pavilion, we'll come to the site of the Sacrificial Hall. The original hall was very large and was used to enshrine Emperor Zhu Yuanzhang and his empress. But the original one was destroyed in the war with 56 stone column bases left, and the present one was rebuilt, twice restored in the Qing Dynasty.

Let's continue our visit. Now, we are going across a big stone bridge. We can see "The Citadel of Treasures and the Tomb Mound". The Citadel of Treasures is the site of graveyard and the Tomb Mound is the tomb itself. The citadel is 39 meters long from west to east and 18 meters wide from north to south. Climb up 54 steps, and coming into our view is the Tomb Mound, which is half circled by a stone wall. In the middle of the wall there are 7 Chinese characters, meaning *The hill is the very tomb of the Ming's founding Emperor*. The tomb is covered by a large mound—400 meters in diameter. Emperor Zhu Yuanzhang and his empress are entombed in the underground. For the technical reasons of preservation, the tomb has not been excavated.

The tomb site was selected by Zhu Yuanzhang himself. However, there had been a Buddhist temple here. Emperor Zhu once paced up and down and looked upset each time when he was here. A wise abbot in the temple took the emperor's cue and suggested that the temple should be moved because his teacher told him so in his dream. The emperor was so happy that he had the temple rebuilt to the east of his tomb. OK, that's the story for the Ming Tomb! Thank you for your attention!

语言储备 Words and Expressions

1. 专业术语   Special Terms

tour arrangement	旅游安排
tour brochure	旅游小手册
tour destination	旅游目的地
parking lot	停车场
gathering time/place	集合时间/地点
entrance ticket	门票
national park	国家公园
theme park	主题公园
summer resort	避暑胜地
Buddhist resort	佛教胜地
Taoist mountain	道教名山
pavilion	亭
lakeside rocks and rockeries	湖石假山
watchtower	角楼
pagoda/tower	塔
terrace	台
altar	坛
pavilion on the water	水榭
pillar/column/post	柱
inscriptions on a tablet	碑刻,碑文,碑铭
the forest of steles/tablet forest	碑林
murals/fresco	壁画
antique/antiquity/curio	古董
antique/curio shop	古玩店
place of historical interest	古迹
ancient architectural(building) complex	古建筑群
ancient tomb	古墓
cave/cavern	洞穴；岩洞
inscriptions on cliffs	摩崖石刻

age-old pine tree	古松
corridor	回廊
winding path	曲径
stream	溪流
waterfall/fall	瀑布
snow-capped mountain	雪山
riverside scenery	水乡景色
natural landscape	自然景观
places of historic figures and cultural heritage	人文景观
commercial attraction	商业景点
World Heritage Sites(WHS)	世界文化遗产保护地
classical Chinese garden	中国古典园林
royal garden	皇家园林
private garden	私家园林
Suzhou Classical Gardens	苏州园林
Summer Palace	颐和园
Yuan-Ming Yuan/Imperial Garden	圆明园
Great Wall	长城
Forbidden City	故宫
Temple of Heaven	天坛
Chengde Imperial Summer Resort	承德避暑山庄
The Museum of Qin Shi Huang Terracotta Warriors and Horses	
	秦始皇兵马俑博物馆
Potala Palace in Lhasa, Tibet	西藏拉萨布达拉宫
Mogao Grottoes at Dunhuang	(甘肃)敦煌莫高窟
Ancient Town of Lijiang	(云南)丽江古城
Ancient City of Pingyao	(山西)平遥古城
Ancient Villages in South Anhui: Xidi and Hongcun	
	安徽古村落：西递、宏村
Dazu Rock Carvings	(重庆)大足石刻
Mount Qingcheng and Dujiang Dam	青城山及都江堰
The Temple, Mansion and Cemetery of Confucius in Qufu	
	曲阜孔庙、孔府、孔林

Mount Tai	泰山
Mount Huang	黄山
Mount Wuyi	武夷山
Mount Emei and the Leshan Giant Buddha	峨眉山及乐山大佛
Sichuan Giant Panda Habitat	四川大熊猫栖息地
Jiuzhaigou Valley	九寨沟

2. 实用句型　Useful Sentences

(1) We will start at 7:00 tomorrow morning from the hotel lobby.
我们明早七点从酒店大堂出发。

(2) It takes an hour to arrive at Nanjing Museum.
到达南京博物馆需要一个小时。

(3) You'll have a good chance to feast your eyes on the Xuanwu Lake.
你们将有机会饱览玄武湖上的美景。

(4) The place is famous(noted/well-known) for its silk and tea.
此地以丝绸和茶叶闻名。

(5) Now we are at the center of the scenic spot.
现在我们在景区的中心位置。

(6) May I have your attention to the mountains in the distance?
请大家注意远处的群山。

(7) This tower boasts the tallest building in Asia.
此塔以亚洲最高的建筑而闻名。

(8) The road runs along the river bank.
这条路顺着河岸延伸。

(9) It is a symbol of Chinese civilization and one of the wonders that the Chinese have created.
这是中华文明的象征,也是中国人民创造的一大奇迹。

(10) The city is a good place to find both historical and natural wonders.
这座城市是个历史底蕴与自然美景共生的宝地。

知识链接 Related Knowledge

导游讲解遵循的"三原则"

导游讲解是导游以丰富多彩的社会生活和璀璨壮丽的自然美景为题材，以兴趣爱好不同、审美情趣各异的游客为对象，对自己掌握的各类知识进行整理、加工和提炼，用简单明快的语言，进行一种意境的再创造。因此，导游讲解技能体现的是多样性、灵活性和创造性。

导游讲解方法和技巧在运用时虽然千差万别，但是都有其内在的基本规律。一般说来，导游在导游活动中必须遵循以下原则：

1. 因人而异

因人而异是指导游应该从游客的实际情况出发，决定讲解内容的深度、广度和重点。面对不同旅游者，导游应该在接待方式、服务形式、导游内容、语言运用、讲解的方式和方法上有所不同。通俗地说，即导游要看人说话、投其所好，讲的正是游客希望知道的、有能力接受的、感兴趣的内容。

2. 因地制宜

因地制宜是指导游应该根据地点的不同，采取不同的导游方法和技巧。对于不同的景点和景观类型、在不同的观赏角度或空间条件变动情况下的同一景点，往往要采用不同的方法和技巧进行导游讲解。

3. 因时而变

导游员必须根据季节的变化及时间的不同，因时而变，灵活地选择导游知识，采用切合实际的方式进行导游讲解。讲解的内容可深可浅、能长能短、可断可续，一切须视具体时空条件而定，切忌千篇一律、墨守成规。

导游讲解的因人而异、因地制宜、因时而变原则体现了导游活动的本质，也反映了导游方法和技巧运用的规律。导游应灵活地运用这三个基本原则，自然而巧妙地将其融入导游讲解之中，不断提高导游讲解水平和导游服务质量。

（《导游服务技能》编写组：《导游服务技能》，中国旅游出版社，2014 年。）

模块六　购物服务

Module 6　Shopping Service

任务描述 Task Description

旅游购物服务是指导游在带领旅游团旅游过程中,对于游客提出的购物要求提供服务所做的工作。其服务主要包括了解游客的购物需求、带领客人购物、对商品进行讨价还价等。

Shopping service means the work the guide does for the tourists when they do shopping during the tour, including learning about the tourists' shopping requirements, taking them to the shop, and bargaining for the tourists, etc.

任务目标 Learning Objectives

1. 帮助游客兑换货币,了解国内传统产品知识并学习购物用语。

Help tourists exchange currency, master the knowledge of traditional Chinese products and produce, and learn shopping expressions in English.

2. 了解相关购物信息,掌握帮助游客讨价还价的技能,并能够帮助游客购买及退换商品。

Learn about the related shopping information, master the skills of bargaining for tourists, and assist tourists in buying goods and returning goods for a refund.

3. 了解如何用英语与游客有效沟通,以及如何带领其购物,并练习帮助游客讨价还价的导游服务技能。

Learn how to communicate in English with the tourists and how to help them in shopping, and practice the skills of bargaining for tourists.

工作流程 Working Process

1. 了解游客的购物需求。

Learn about the tourists' shopping requirements.

2. 帮助游客兑换本地货币。

Help the tourists exchange currency when necessary.

3. 带领游客前往经过旅游管理机构认证的商场购物。

Lead the tourists to the shops which have been approved by the Tourism Bureau.

4. 向商店营业员询问游客想要购买的产品的情况。

Get information from the shop assistant about the products and produce the tourists would like to buy.

5. 帮助游客选择商品。

Help the tourists choose items.

6. 帮助游客询问价格。

Ask about prices for tourists.

7. 帮助游客对商品进行讨价还价。

Bargain for the tourists with shop assistants.

8. 帮助游客购买商品。

Give help to the tourists in buying the goods they need.

9. 帮助游客付款并索要相关购物凭证以备海关验证通行。

Help the tourists make payment, and ask the store for official receipts in case the customs asks for them.

10. 当所购商品出现问题时,帮助游客退换货物。

Assist the tourists in returning or changing goods when necessary.

小贴士 Tips

旅游购物学问多

出门在外,买点地方特产和纪念品之类,体验异地消费情趣,是游客的普遍心理。怎样在旅途中购物,可是一门学问。

1. 以地方特色为取舍

地方特色商品不仅具有纪念意义,而且正宗,有价格优势,值得

消费者购买。如杭州的龙井茶、海南的椰子、云南的民族服饰、西藏的哈达等,购买后留作纪念或送给亲朋好友,都是不错的选择。

2. 以小型轻便为首选

有些特色商品体积笨重庞大,随身携带很不方便,不宜购买。人在旅途,游山玩水、乘坐车船并不轻松,行李越少越好。有些物品还可能易碎,稍不小心就会中途摔坏,不必为此花冤枉钱。

3. 切忌贪便宜

在某些风景区,经常有兜售假冒伪劣商品的,如珍珠、项链、茶叶之类,游客要经得住价格和叫卖的诱惑。有时自以为捡了便宜,回来后经过一番鉴别,结果大呼上当,退货、调换几乎不可能。

4. 相信自己的判断

政府对旅游业有严格的监管,大部分导游都能遵守职业道德,但是,仍有少数导游受利益的驱动会想尽办法把团队拉到给回扣的商店,任意延长购物时间,乐此不疲地为游客介绍、选购物品。对此,游客还是要有提防心理,要增强自我保护意识。在异地购物不要盲目轻信别人,切忌冲动从众,要管住自己的钱袋,做理性的消费者。

课堂实训　In-class Practice

实训项目1　Task 1

情景对话：了解客人购物需求

Dialogue：Learning about the Tourists' Shopping Needs

实训要求：导游龚先生和游客们回到了上海世纪皇冠假日酒店的住处,龚先生告诉游客们晚上自由活动。游客帕克先生想给自己的亲友买一些当地特产,向导游龚先生咨询。

Directions：Mr. Gong, the local guide and the tourists arrive at Shanghai Crowne Plaza Century Park back from a scenic spot. He is telling the tourists that they are free in the evening. A tourist, Mr. Parker, wants to buy some souvenirs for his family and friends, so he is seeking advice from Mr. Gong.

示例　**Model**

（G：local guide，Mr. Gong　P：tourist，Mr. Parker）

G：Attention，please. Today's tour is over now. You're free this evening according to the itinerary.

P：Mr. Gong，I want to buy some souvenirs for my family and my friends，could you please introduce to me something famous here in Shanghai?

G：Of course. If you want to buy some famous food here，the Shanghai Sliced Cold Chicken is your best choice. And also in some arts and crafts stores，there is Shanghai Wood Carving.

P：Shanghai Wood Carving sounds nice.

G：OK. I know a famous arts and crafts store for foreign tourists. Shall we go to it now?

P：Wonderful. Thank you for your kindness.

G：My pleasure.

（陈昕：《旅游英语》，人民邮电出版社，2011 年。）

实训项目2　Task 2

实用写作：填写外汇兑换水单

Writing：Filling in an Exchange Memo

实训要求：一位韩国游客想兑换一些钱，但是不知道如何填写外汇水单，导游龚先生帮他填写外汇水单。

Directions：A tourist from Korea wants to exchange some money，but he does not know how to fill out the exchange memo. He is asking tour guide，Mr. Gong for help.

示例　**Model**

（T：tourist　G：local guide，Mr. Gong）

T：Good morning，sir. I am from Korea. My English is poor. Can you help me?

G：It's my pleasure. What's your problem?

T：Oh，I want to exchange some money，but I do not know how to fill out the exchange memo. Here it is. My name is Woo Suk.

G：Good. Could you please tell me your passport number?

T：GN0869747.

G：OK. Mr. Woo Suk, how much do you want to exchange?

T：500,000 KEW.

G：OK. I was wondering if you had ever thought of conversing the unused RMB back into KEW later?

T：Yes, if I have RMB left.

G：So, please keep your exchange memo safe.

T：Thank you very much. I will do it.

G：Not at all.

兑换水单

EXCHANGE MEMO

国籍 Nationality： ＿＿＿＿＿＿＿			护照号码 Passport No.：＿＿＿＿＿＿	
姓名(签名)Name (signature)：＿＿＿＿＿			地址 Address：＿＿＿＿＿＿	
外币金额 **Amount in** **Foreign Currency**	**扣贴息** **Less Discount**	**净额** **Net Amount**	**汇率** **Rate**	**人民币净额** **Net Amount** **（￥yuan）**
注意：请妥善保管此单,持有人可以在六个月内离开中国时将部分未使用的人民币凭本人护照及兑换水单兑换成外币；兑换水单有效期为六个月。 Particulars：Please keep this carefully, part of unused RMB can be reconverted into foreign currency with your passport and the EXCHANGE MEMO when the holder leaves China within six months；the EXCHANGE MEMO is invalid after six months.				
日期 Date：＿＿＿＿＿＿＿		银行办理人 Bank Clerk：＿＿＿＿＿＿		

实训项目3　Task 3

情景对话：购物

Dialogue：Shopping

实训要求：贝克先生想要为妻子买一件礼物,于是他请导游龚先生帮他去商店挑选礼物并帮助他讨价还价。

Directions：Mr. Baker wants to buy a gift for his wife. His tour guide Mr. Gong is helping him in a store, selecting the gift and bargaining with the shop assistant.

示例 Model

（G: local guide, Mr. Gong B: Mr. Baker A: shop assistant）

A: Good evening, sir. What can I do for you?

G: Excuse me, can you recommend a gift for a 40-year-old madam?

A: It's my pleasure. How about Qipao? Woman of that age may be fond of it.

B: Yes, that's a nice gift.

G: How much is it?

A: $ 120.

G: What a price!

A: The price is fair. It's made of silk. Feel it and you will know it is worth the money. It looks wonderful.

G: Any discount?

A: At most 10%.

G: How about 20%?

A: Oh, no. It is in hot sale.

G: OK, you've got it. (to Mr. Baker) It costs $ 108. Will you take it?

B: OK. I'll take it anyway. Here is $ 110. Keep the change.

A: Thank you! Have a nice day!

小贴士 Tips

旅游购物须知

1. 货比三家不吃亏。购买高价物品时,宜多比较,大部分的物品在购买后不可以退货。购买时别忘了索取正规的销售凭证。

2. 您所购买的珠宝宜随身携带而不得以邮寄的方式出境。

3. 勿接受陌生人所提供的导购等服务。

4. 选择各地的超市购物,价格较为合理且可获得品质保证。

5. 尊重地区特殊的宗教信仰,但也要预防以宗教信仰为借口被迫购物。

（http://tools.2345.com/zhishi/changshi/195154.htm.）

课后实训　After-class Practice

实训项目　Task

情景对话：购物

Dialogue： Shopping

实训要求：安妮丽想要为妹妹买一件礼物，但她发现自己拿不定主意。作为她的导游，向她推荐旗袍，并说明推荐理由。

Directions： Annelie wants to buy something for her sister but she finds that it is hard to make a choice. You are her guide and recommend to her Qipao (cheongsam). You talk about the reasons for your recommendation.

示例　Model

（G：local guide, Mr. Gong　A：Annelie）

G：Good morning, Annelie. What can I do for you?

A：Excuse me, I want to buy something for my sister, but you know it's hard for me to make a choice. Can you recommend something for me?

G：It's my pleasure. How about Qipao? Women may like it.

A：What's that for?

G：Qipao or cheongsam is a female dress with distinctive Chinese features and enjoys a growing popularity in the international world of high fashion.

A：That sounds nice! What is it made of?

G：It is usually made of silk.

A：That's very good. I'll take it. Can you show me the way to the shop where I can buy it?

G：Sure, it's my pleasure.

语言储备 Words and Expressions

1. 专业术语　Special Terms

hypermarket/mass merchandiser	量贩店,大卖场
department store	百货商店
shopping mall	购物中心
supermarket	超市
convenience store	便利店
grocery store	杂货店
discount store	折扣店
pharmacy/drugstore	药店
cosmetic outlet	化妆品批发店
dime store	廉价商店
Chinese knot	中国结
paper cut	剪纸
silk scarf	丝巾
Tang costume	唐装
Beijing Opera mask	京剧脸谱
Guizhou Maotai	贵州茅台(酒)
Suzhou embroidery	苏绣
Jingdezhen porcelain wares	景德镇瓷(器)
tri-colored glazed pottery of the Tang Dynasty	唐三彩
cloisonné; cloisonné enamel	景泰蓝
Suzhou sandalwood fan	苏州檀香扇
ink painting	水墨画
bronze ware	青铜器
artifact; handicraft	手工艺品
traditional Chinese painting	国画
clay figure modeling	泥塑

2. 实用句型　Useful Sentences

(1) Can I help you? /What can I do for you? /Anything I can do for you?

请问你要买点什么?

(2) I'd like to buy a gift for my wife.

我想给我妻子买个礼物。

(3) Nothing, thank you. I'm just looking round.

不用,谢谢,我自己看看。

(4) —Would you mind/care if I try this on?

我可以试穿一下吗?

—Not at all. /Certainly not. /Of course not. /Not in the least.

没问题。

(5) I'm sorry/I'm afraid that you can't try it on.

很抱歉,这个不能试穿。

(6) —What color/style/brand/material do you prefer/like/want to buy?

你想买什么颜色/样式/品牌/材料的?

—I prefer/like green/ordinary style/Adidas Brand/cotton.

我想买绿色/普通样式/阿迪达斯/棉质的。

(7) It amounts to/It comes to/It is 300 yuan in all.

一共三百元。

(8) Can you give me a little deal on this? / Can you give me this for cheaper?

这能卖得便宜一点吗?

(9) Is there any discount on bulk purchases?

我多买些能打折吗?

(10) Give me a discount.

给我打个折吧。

(11) How much do you want for this?

这件东西你想卖多少钱?

(12) If you don't give me a better price, I won't buy this.

如果价格不更优惠些,我是不会买的。

知识链接 Related Knowledge

国家旅游局关于打击旅游活动中欺骗、强制购物行为的意见

(旅发〔2015〕217 号)

购物是旅游活动的重要组成部分,是规范旅游市场秩序的关键环节。"欺骗、强制旅游购物"已严重损害旅游者权益,深为人民群众诟病。为进一步明确旅行社及从业人员、购物场所和旅游者的责任和义务,大力整治"欺骗、强制旅游购物",现提出以下意见。

一、"欺骗、强制旅游购物"行为的认定

有以下行为之一,可被认定为"欺骗、强制旅游购物":一是旅行社未经旅游者书面同意,安排购物的;二是旅行社、导游领队对旅游者进行人身威胁、恐吓等行为强迫旅游者购物的;三是旅行社、导游领队安排的购物场所属于非法营业或者未向社会公众开放的;四是旅行社、导游领队安排的购物场所销售商品掺杂、掺假,以假充真、以次充好,以不合格产品冒充合格产品的;五是旅行社、导游领队明知或者应知安排的购物场所的经营者有严重损害旅游者权益记录的;六是旅行社、导游领队收取购物场所经营者回扣等不正当利益的;七是购物场所经营者存在《消费者权益保护法》第五十六条规定情形的;八是法津、法规规定的旅行社、导游领队及购物场所经营者通过安排购物损害旅游者合法权益的其他行为。

二、对"欺骗、强制旅游购物"违法行为的处罚处理标准

各级旅游部门按以下标准依法对"欺骗、强制旅游购物"违法行为进行处罚处理:

(一)对旅行社的处罚处理:一是没收违法所得,责令停业整顿三个月,情节严重的,吊销旅行社业务经营许可证;二是处三十万元罚款,违法所得三十万元以上的,处违法所得五倍罚款;三是列入旅游经营服务不良信息,并转入旅游经营服务信用档案,向社会公布。

(二)对旅行社相关责任人的处罚处理:一是对直接负责主管人员和其他直接责任人员,没收违法所得,处二万元罚款;二是被吊销旅行社业务经营许可证的旅行社法人代表和主要管理人员,自处罚之日起未逾三年的,不得从事旅行社业务;三是列入旅游经营服务不良信息,并转入旅游经营服务信用档案,向社会予以公布。

(三)对导游、领队的处罚处理:一是没收违法所得,处二万元罚款,并吊销导游证、领队证;二是被吊销导游证、领队证的导游、领队,自处罚之日起未逾三年的,不得重新申请导游证、领队证;三是列入旅游经营服务不良信息,并转入旅游经营服务信用档案,向社会予以公布。

(四)对购物场所及其经营者的处理:一是列入旅游经营服务不良信息,并转入旅游经营服务信用档案,向社会予以公布;二是要求旅行社及其从业人员不得带旅游者进入被列入旅游经营服务信用档案名单的购物

场所；三是依法移送公安、工商等相关部门。

三、工作要求

（一）各地要督促旅行社诚信经营、提升品质，加强部门和分支机构及导游领队的管理，审慎选择购物场所，并与其签订合同，明确产品服务质量及责任，抵制"欺骗、强制旅游购物"行为，使用国家旅游局与国家工商总局制定的合同范本，载明旅游购物场所的基本信息，提示可能存在的消费风险。

（二）各地要加大对导游领队的培训教育，引导广大导游领队用辛勤劳动、诚实劳动创造美好生活，自觉提高自身素质和服务水平，主动举报旅行社、购物场所的"欺骗、强制旅游购物"行为。

（三）各地要通过媒体合作，加大对旅游者的宣传教育，引导旅游者理性消费、理性维权，与旅行社签订正规的旅游合同，拒绝签订旅行社提供的虚假旅游合同，主动索要团费和购物发票，积极举报旅行社、导游领队、购物场所经营者的违法违规行为。

（四）各级旅游部门要严格执行意见要求，要针对问题多发的旅游市场，加大对"欺骗、强制旅游购物"的打击力度，主动协调公安、工商、商务等部门，加强联合执法，共同净化旅游购物环境，推动旅游业可持续发展。

（http://www.cnta.gov.cn/zwgk/tzggnew/201509/t20150930.748255.shtml.）

模块七　送团服务

Module 7　Seeing off a Tour Group

任务描述 Task Description

送团服务,是指旅游团结束一地参观游览活动后,导游为使游客顺利、安全离开而做的送行工作。导游的送团服务主要包括临行前的业务准备、离店服务、送行服务和后续工作。

Seeing off service refers to the work the tour guide does after the tour group end up their tour to ensure them a safe and sound journey back. It includes preparations before departure, checking out at the hotel, going with the tourists to the station, airport, or port and bidding farewell to them and the follow-up work.

任务目标 Learning Objectives

1. 掌握送团工作的主要内容和送团服务的标准流程;熟悉离店手续;掌握欢送辞的编写和表达。

Master the main contents and procedures of the service of seeing off a tour group. Get familiarized with hotel checking out. Know how to write and make a farewell speech.

2. 能专业化地实施送团流程;熟悉相关表达,使用英语熟练开展送团工作。

Work professionally following the procedures of seeing off a tour group. Master the words and expressions concerned to communicate in English with foreign tourists in departure.

3. 培养耐心细致的工作态度和热情真诚的服务意识。

Develop an attitude of working patiently and carefully, and raise an awareness of serving the tourists sincerely and enthusiastically.

工作流程 Working Process

1. 做好临行前准备

Make preparations before departure.

（1）核实交通票据

Double check the transport tickets.

① 在旅游团离开前一天，做好游客离开所需交通票据的核实工作。

The day before the tour group leaving, make sure that the required tickets, documents and the alike are all ready for the tour group's departure.

② 核对旅游团团名、代号、人数、领队及全程导游姓名、航班(车次、船次)、机场(车站、码头)、离开及到达的时间等信息。

Double check the written information such as the name and the code of the tour group, number of the tourists, names of the national guide and the tour leader, the flight (train, ship) number, airport (station, wharf), and time of departure and arrival.

③ 核实旅游团的具体交通方式和出发时间，具体要核对计划时间、时刻表、票面时间和问询时间。

Confirm the tour group's transportation means and departure time. To be more specific, check the planning time, the schedule of transport, the time on the ticket and the time from the information inquiry.

④ 弄清启程机场(车站、码头)位置，如班次有变更，应及时汇报，并提醒全程导游向下一站交代有关情况。

Confirm the position of the airport (station, wharf). Timely report is needed if transport change occurs. Remind the national guide to send all the information to the next stop.

（2）商定好出发事宜

Agree on departing matters.

① 与全程导游、领队商定集中和出发时间，告知旅游者。

Discuss gathering and departure time with the national guide and the tour leader, and inform the tourists of your decision.

② 商定好出行李时间后,提前通知酒店负责行李服务的相关人员,以便其能及时提供相应服务。

Agree on the time for luggage pickup, and then get in touch with the luggage service staff in advance so that the latter can give timely service.

③ 与全程导游和领队确定叫早和早饭时间,并告知游客和酒店相关部门。

Discuss with the tour leader and the national guide, and decide on the time of the next day's morning call and breakfast. Inform tourists as well as the related section of the hotel.

(3) 及时归还证件。旅游团出发前一天,归还游客证件、票据等。

Return to the tourists their ID cards, passports, papers, tickets and the like one day prior to their departure.

2. 办理退房手续

Check out.

(1) 行李确认和交接

Check and turn over the luggage.

① 退房前,按商定的时间与全程导游和领队共同检查行李是否上锁、捆扎,有无破损等,清点、确认行李件数。

Together with the national guide and the tour leader, confirm the number of pieces of luggage to be delivered, check to make sure that every piece is locked and packed well, and that there is no damage.

② 与酒店行李员完成行李交接,填写行李交运卡。

Handle the luggage turnover procedure with the bellman, and fill out luggage delivery forms.

(2) 协助旅客退房

Help tourists with the check-out.

① 提醒游客结清全部费用,包括酒水、饮料、一次性用品及电话费等杂费。

Remind the tourists to settle accounts for incidental expenses with the hotel, including bills of drinks, beverages, disposable items, telephone charges, etc.

② 协助办理退房手续,并询问游客是否已结清账目。

Help tourists with the check-out, and ask whether they have cleared the bills.

(3) 集合登车

Gather to get on the bus.

① 出发前,提醒游客不要遗漏行李物品,并组织游客上车。

Before setting off, remind the tourists to check if they forget or leave behind anything. Gather all the tourists to get on the bus.

② 待游客放好随身物品入座后,认真清点实到人数。

When the tourists put their carry-on in place and are seated, check carefully to make sure no tourist is left behind.

③ 全体到齐后,再次提醒游客检查随身物品,如无遗漏,在征询领队意见后,示意司机出发。

When all the tourists are on the bus, remind them to double check their belongings. When everything is OK, get the tour leader's consent and ask the driver to set off.

3. 给游客送行

See the tourists off.

(1) 在去机场(车站、码头)的路上,向全体游客致欢送辞。

Make a farewell speech on the way to the airport(station, wharf).

(2) 请全程导游、领队或游客代表填写旅游团意见征询表。

Give out the feedback forms and ask for opinions and advice concerning the service, from the national guide, the tour leader or the tourist representatives.

(3) 到达机场(车站、码头)后,照顾游客下车,提醒游客带齐随身行李物品,以及必要的证件和文件。

When arriving at the airport (station, wharf), help the tourists to get off, and remind them to take all their belongings and required certificates or documents with them.

(4) 请领队、全程导游一起与行李员交接行李,清点检查后交给游客。

Together with the leader and the national guide, deal with the handover of luggage with the bellman, check and give back all the luggage to the tourists.

(5) 协助全程导游和领队办理登机和其他离站手续。

Help the national guide and the tour leader deal with check-in and other departure procedures.

(6) 当游客进入安检口后,再离开。与游客告别,祝其旅途顺利。

Don't leave until the tourists enter the security check area, bid farewell to the tourists, and wish them a good journey.

4. 完成后续工作

Complete the follow-up work.

（1）如有旅客委托事宜,尽快按程序办理;确因困难办不成或不能尽快办成则需向游客说明原因。

If there is anything entrusted by tourists, deal with it quickly as required. If it cannot be done or some delay is unavoidable due to some difficulties, explain to the tourist as soon as possible.

（2）整理旅游过程中发生的账目票据和表单,与财务部门结清所有账目。归还从旅行社借出的耳麦、导游旗等物品。

Sort out the accounts and receipts of the tour, and clear all the bills. Return such supplies borrowed from the travel agency as the loudspeaker, banner, etc.

（3）整理带团记录,若旅游过程中发生较为严重的旅游事故,则需有书面材料向旅行社领导汇报。

Sort out the working notes. If there is any serious accident during the tour, report it to the head of the agency in written form.

（4）做好带团总结,吸取成功经验和失败教训,以不断提高服务质量。

Make a summary of the entire work. Learn from successes and failures to improve future work.

小贴士 Tips

致欢送辞

欢送辞主要包含六大内容：表示惜别、感谢合作、小结旅游、征求意见、期盼重逢、预祝客人一路顺风。要强调真情自然流露,点到即可,切记不可过分渲染,给人虚假之嫌。工作中如有疏漏,感谢合作时可先表示歉意以消除游客怨气,表明诚意;如果团队旅行顺利完美,感谢合作则能起到锦上添花的作用。导游可视时间长短,带领游客回忆游览项目和参加的活动,一起归纳总结,并将感性认识上升到理性认识,使游客留下深刻印象。最后,导游要提醒游客不要落下东西,祝愿游客旅途平安,并期盼再相逢。

课堂实训　In-class Practice

实训项目 1　Task 1

情景对话：送站准备

Dialogue：Preparations before Departure

实训要求：来自澳大利亚的 18 人旅游团即将完成此次北京—西安—南京—上海的中国十日之旅，今天晚上即将从上海浦东国际机场返程。请以地接导游的身份和领队核实有关票据、集中时间、地点等送站准备事宜。

Directions：The Australian tour group of 18 persons is going to end up the 10-day tour in China, a tour of Beijing, Xi'an, Nanjing and Shanghai, and is going to go back to Australia tomorrow evening. You, the local tour guide, discuss with the national leader about such preparations before the departure as flight tickets, the time and place of gathering, etc.

示例　Model

（G：local guide, Mr. Gong Yanling　L：tour leader, Mr. Ginpil）

(1)

G：Hi, Mr. Ginpil, you are leaving for home tomorrow evening.

L：Yes. How time flies! I can't believe tomorrow will be the last day of my tour in China.

G：Time surely flies when you are having fun. But right now, I have to remind you of something. Have you confirmed all your flight tickets yet?

L：Oh, yes. As soon as you reminded me of that yesterday, I asked the hotel reception desk to confirm them for us.

G：Great. So I would confirm again that you are leaving to Sydney by CA1 ** at 21：30 on June 15 from Shanghai Pudong International Airport. Am I right?

L：Exactly.

（2）

L：So what time shall we leave for the airport?

G：Well, according to the latest service standard, for an international flight, the passengers would better arrive at the airport at least three hours before the departure time and it is about 30 minutes' ride from our hotel, to the airport. By the way, do you still remember the departure time of your flight?

L：It's at 21:30 tomorrow evening.

G：Right. In that case, we will leave for Shanghai Pudong International Airport at 17:30 tomorrow afternoon. I will wait for you in the lobby at 17:20 and a bus will pick us up.

L：Fine. Let's meet in the lobby then.

（3）

G：By the way, it will be appreciated if you can go through the check-out formality and get the luggage ready before that time.

L：No problem. What else should I do?

G：Please put your travel documents, flight tickets, and declaration items in your carry-on bag. It will be much more convenient for you to check in and go through the Customs at the airport.

L：You are so considerate, thank you for your reminding. So, I will tell all that to the other members of our tour group. See you tomorrow.

G：Ok. See you. I wish you all a good time for your last night in China.

L：Thank you very much.

G：My pleasure!

实训项目2 Task 2

情景对话：送站安排

Dialogue：Departure Arrangements

实训要求：来自澳大利亚的18人旅游团结束了所有行程,今天晚上即将返程。领队召集了团队成员,请以地接导游的身份告知游客具体时间安排等事项。

Directions：The tour group of 18 people from Australia has finished their tour, and is going back this evening. After the tour leader gathers all the tour group members, you, the local tour guide, inform them of the arrangements and schedule for departure.

示例　Model

（G: local guide, Gong Yanling　L: tour leader, Mr. Ginpil）

L: Attention, please. Our tour guide, Mr. Gong has something to say. Let's listen to him carefully.

G: Ladies and gentlemen, now I'd like to say something about today's departure arrangements. First, we will count the pieces of the luggage to be checked. Please put your luggage outside the door of your room before 17:10 this afternoon. The bellman will collect your luggage. Second, since the departure time of our flight is at 21:30 this evening, we have to set off at 17:30. I hope everyone will be on the bus by then. Third, if you have any RMB with you, you'd better convert it back into Australian dollars at the bank at the airport. Please check out for your incidentals ahead of time, since we cannot afford to be late this afternoon. If your luggage is overweight, be prepared to pay for the overweight. If you have something to declare, you have to fill in the customs declaration form. Last but not the least, please make sure that you have your air ticket and passport with you at hand. If you have any questions, do not hesitate to let me know. Any questions? Thanks for your time. Hope you have a happy journey home.

实训项目3　Task 3

情景对话：退房

Dialogue：Check-out

实训要求：澳大利亚旅游团即将启程返回。请两人一组,分饰地接导游和收银员完成退房手续。

Directions：The Australian tour group is going to leave. Please play the roles of the local tour guide and the hotel cashier, and go through the check out formality in the form of a conversation in pairs.

实训材料：房卡或房门钥匙、账单、现金、信用卡、发票

Props：room cards or keys, bills, some cash, credit card, receipts

示例　**Model**

（C：hotel cashier　G：local guide, Mr. Gong Yanling）

C：Good afternoon, sir. May I help you?

G：Yes, I'd like to settle the bill for our group.

C：OK. May I have your name and room numbers?

G：Gong Yanling, tour guide from SH ＊＊ Travel Service. We stay in Room 8011 to Room 8019, nine rooms altogether.

C：May I have your room keys, please?

G：Sure. Here you are.

C：Just a moment, please. I'll have the bill ready for you. (after a while) Thank you for waiting. Your bill totals 3800 Yuan.

G：That much? Would you mind letting me have a look at it?

C：Not at all, sir. Here you are.

G：Thanks. Well, it seems to be right.

C：How would you like to make that payment?

G：By credit card. Here you are.

C：Just a moment, please. I'll write out our receipt for you. Here is your receipt. I'll send a porter to pick up your baggage.

G：Thank you.

实训项目4　Task 4

情景表演：致欢送辞

Acting：Making a Farewell Speech

实训要求：澳大利亚旅游团结束全部行程，正在赶往浦东机场的途中。请以地接导游的身份向旅游团致欢送辞。

Directions：The Australian tour group has finished the tour in China, and is on their way to Shanghai Pudong International Airport. Please make a farewell speech to the tourists.

示例　**Model**

Ladies and gentlemen：

　　Your visit in China is drawing to a close. I hate to do this, but I still have to say goodbye to you all. It has been the most wonderful experience for me to be with you all the way. I hope you have enjoyed your stay here in China. If there is anything you are not satisfied with, please do not hesitate to tell me so that I can do better in my future work. Here, I'd like to take this opportunity to thank you all for your understanding and cooperation. I sincerely hope that you'll come to China again. Hope to see you again and to be your guide once more.

Once again, thank you for your support and cooperation.

小贴士 Tips

抵达须知

如果游客乘坐火车、轮船离开，要求提前 1 小时抵达车站、码头；如果乘坐国内航班，要求提前 2 小时抵达机场；如果乘坐出境航班，则要求提前 3 小时抵达机场。游客到达机场、车站、码头前，导游应提醒游客带齐随身行李物品，到达后导游应最先下车并站立于车门前侧引导协助游客下车，并检查车内有无游客遗漏物品。在办理相关手续时，应安顿好游客让他们在一个集中位置等候，并再次提醒游客保管好随身物品。

课后实训　After-class Practice

实训项目 1　Task 1

情景对话：退房

Dialogue：Checking Out at the Hotel

实训要求：王敏是一名游客，正要离开酒店。张婷是酒店的收银员，为她办理退房手续。

Directions：Wang Min is a tourist and is leaving the hotel. Zhang Ting is a cashier in a hotel. Check her out properly.

示例　Model

（Z：hotel cashier, Zhang Ting　W：tourist, Wang Min）

Z：Good morning, Miss. What can I do for you?

W：Yes, I'd like to check out now.

Z：What's your name and room number, please?

W：Wang Min, Room 818.

Z：May I have your room card, please?

W：Yes. Here you are.

Z：Thank you. Has all the luggage been taken out of the room?

W：Yes. All the bags have already been loaded on to the shuttle bus.

Z：Fine. The bill adds up to 480 Yuan.

W：May I check it?

Z：By all means.

W：What is this charge here?

Z：That's for the long-distance call you made this morning.

W：I see. Is credit card OK?

Z：Sorry, Miss. We only accept cash.

W：All right. Here you are.

Z：Please sign your name here.

W：Oh, yes.

Z：Here is your receipt. Welcome to come again.

W：Thank you. Bye-bye.

Z：Bye.

实训项目2 Task 2

情景表演：致欢送辞

Acting：Making a Farewell Speech

实训要求：澳大利亚文化旅游团结束了全部行程,明天早晨返回澳洲家乡。你是导游小龚,请给旅游团致欢送辞。

Directions：The tourists of the Australian Cultural Tour Group have finished their tour, and are leaving for their homes in Australia tomorrow morning. You are tour guide Gong. Please make a farewell speech to them.

示例 Model

Ladies and Gentlemen,

Time goes by so quickly and your trip in Shanghai is drawing to a close. Tomorrow morning you will be leaving Shanghai by air and going back home. On behalf of China ✳✳ Travel Service Shanghai branch and my Chinese colleagues here, I'd like to express our heartfelt thanks and bid farewell to our Australian friends. Thank you for your patience and friendliness, which has made our work easier and enabled us to learn much about your country. We also appreciate your cooperation and understanding, which has made the trip a pleasure and success.

Any way we have to say goodbye to each other now, and I wish we'd meet when you come to China next time. Have a nice day and a pleasant trip.

语言储备 Words and Expressions

1. 专业术语　Special Terms

receipt	收据
invoice	发票
transfer	转账
credit card	信用卡
credit limit	信用卡额度
room charge	房费
service charge	服务费
incidentals	杂费
phone charge	电话费
laundry charge	洗衣费
food bill	餐费账单
settle the bill	付账
exchange rate	汇率
cash	现金
carry-on	手提行李,随身行李
overweight	超重的
aircraft	飞机；飞行器
round-trip ticket	往返票
one-way ticket	单程票
half-price ticket	半票
accident insurance	意外保险
travel insurance	旅行平安保险

check-in counter	办理登机手续服务台
customs declaration	海关申报
customs declaration form	海关申报表
goods to declare	申报物品
passport control	护照检查
disembarkation card	入境卡
departure card	出境卡
vaccination certificate	防疫证书
Health Certificate for International Travelers	国际旅行健康证明书
security check	安全检查
detector	探测器
dangerous articles	危险物品
duty-free shop	免税店
departure lounge	候机室
boarding /departure gate	登机口
boarding pass/card	登机牌
first class	头等舱
business class	商务舱
economy class	经济舱
flight attendant	客机上的服务人员
steward	男乘务员
stewardess	女乘务员
overhead bin/compartment	（座位上方）行李舱
seat number	座位号
aisle seat	靠过道座位
window seat	靠窗座位
seat belt	安全带
air-sickness bag	呕吐袋
seat pocket	座位袋
emergency exit	紧急出口
lavatory/toilet	洗手间
life vest/life jacket	救生衣
oxygen mask	氧气罩

occupied	（有人）使用中
vacant	无人使用

2. 实用句型　Useful Sentences

（1）What we have arranged is that the tour group will gather together at 9：00 a.m. in front of the Shangri-La Hotel and take the bus to the railway station.

我们的安排是早上 9 点在香格里拉酒店门前集中，然后再乘坐大巴去火车站。

（2）I am regretful that we can't change the time because it has been made by the local travel agency.

非常抱歉，这个时间是由当地旅行社决定的，我们无法更改。

（3）I'm in Room 8018. I'm leaving today. Please settle my account.

我住 8018 房间，打算今天离开，请结账。

（4）I'm leaving early tomorrow morning. Please have my bill ready.

我明天一早离开，请把账结好。

（5）I'll be checking out at 8：00 a.m. Where can I pay my bill?

我打算早上 8 点退房，请问在哪儿结账？

（6）Have you used any hotel service facilities or had breakfast at the hotel dining room this morning?

请问您今天早上是否用过酒店内的服务设施，或在酒店餐厅用过早餐？

（7）Three nights at 400 Yuan each, and six meals you had at the hotel. That makes a total of 1650 Yuan.

3 个晚上，每晚 400 元，酒店用餐 6 餐，总共是 1650 元。

（8）Does this include service?

包含服务费了吗？

（9）It's 650 Yuan, including the phone and laundry charges.

总共 650 元，包含了电话费和洗衣费。

（10）How would you like to pay the bill?

您打算如何付款？

（11）In cash. /By credit card. /By check.

付现金/用信用卡付/用支票付。

（12）May I have an invoice?

可以给我开张发票吗？

（13）Here's your change and receipt.

这是您的零钱和收据。

（14）Please confirm your bill and sign your name here.

请您签字确认账单。

（15）Have a safe trip!

祝您一路平安！

（16）Wish you a pleasant journey! Good luck.

祝您旅途愉快！祝您好运！

（17）We look forward to serving you again.

期待再次为您服务。

（18）Hope to meet you in Shanghai again.

希望能再次在上海见到您。

知识链接 Related Knowledge

入出境知识

1. 入境

外国人、华侨、港澳台同胞及中国公民自海外入境或返归，均须在指定的口岸向边防检查站（由公安、海关、卫生检疫三方组成）交验有效证件，填写入境卡，经边防检查站检验核准加盖验讫章后方可入境。

（1）护照

护照是一国主管机关发给本国公民出国或在国外居留的证件，证明其国籍和身份。护照一般分外交护照、公务护照和普通护照三种。

① 外交护照。发给政府高级官员、国会议员、外交和领事官员、负有特殊外交使命的人员、政府代表团成员等。持有外交护照者在外国享受外交礼遇（如豁免权）。

② 公务护照。发给政府官员与驻外使、领馆工作人员，以及因公派注国外执行文化、经济等任务的人员。

③ 普通护照。发给出国的一般公民、国外侨民。

在中国，外交、公务护照由外事部门颁发，普通护照由公安部门颁发。中华人民共和国护照的有效期为护照持有人未满16周岁的5年，16周岁以上的

10年。

（2）签证

签证是一国主管机关在本国或外国公民所持的护照或其他旅行证上签注、盖印，表示准其出入本国国境或者过境的手续。华侨回国探亲、旅游无须办理签证。签证分为外交签证、礼遇签证、公务签证、普通签证等。还可分为入境签证、入出境签证、出入境签证。旅游签证属于普通签证，在中国为"L"字签证（发给来中国旅游、探亲或因其他私人事务入境的人员）。签证上规定有持证在中国停留的起止日期。9人以上的旅游团可发给团体签证。团体签证一式三份，签发机关留一份，来华旅游团两份，一份用于入境，一份用于出境。签证的有效期不等，获签证者必须在有效期内进入中国境内，超过期限则签证不再有效。持联程票搭乘国际航班直接过境，在中国停留不超过24小时不出机场的外国人免办签证；要求临时离开机场的，需经边防检查机关批准。随着国际关系的改善和旅游事业的发展，许多国家间签订了互免签证协议。

（3）港澳居民来往内地通行证

《港澳居民来往内地通行证》由中华人民共和国公安部出入境管理局签发，是拥有中华人民共和国国籍的香港特别行政区及澳门特别行政区居民来往中国内地所用的证件。通行证的有效期分为5年和10年。申请人年满18周岁的，签发10年有效通行证；未满18周岁的，签发5年有效通行证。香港居民可亲身到香港中国旅行社办理。澳门居民可亲身前往澳门中国旅行社办理。

（4）台湾居民来往大陆通行证

《台湾居民来往大陆通行证》，简称"台胞证"，是台湾地区居民往来大陆地区所持有的证件，由中华人民共和国公安部出入境管理局签发。台湾居民从香港、澳门地区来大陆的，可以向外交部驻香港、澳门特派员公署领事部，香港、澳门中国旅行社申请；台湾居民事先未在境外办妥有效证件及签注而来大陆的，可以向经授权的口岸公安机关出入境管理机构申请；台湾居民从澳门地区参加短期团体旅游珠江三角洲的，可以向授权的广东省公安厅珠海签证办事处申请；福建省福州、厦门市公安机关可通过代办旅行社受理台湾金门、马祖、澎湖地区居民5年有效《台湾居民来往大陆通行证》和签注申请。通行证有效期5年。

2. 出境

（1）外国游客出境

外国游客应当在签证准予停留的期限内从指定口岸出境。外国游客出境，须向口岸边防检查站交验有效护照或者其他有效证件。

不准出境的几种人：

① 刑事案件的被告人和公安机关、人民检察院或法院认定的犯罪嫌疑人；

② 人民法院通知有未了结民事案件不能离境的；

③ 有其他违反中国法津的行为尚未处理，经有关主管机关认定需要追究的。

下列人士，边防检查机关有权限制出境：

① 持无效出境证件的；

② 持伪造、涂改或他人护照、证件的；

③ 拒绝接受查验证件的。

外国游客携带我国文物出境（包括古旧图书、字画等），应向海关递交中国文物管理部门的出口许可证明，不能提供证明的不准携带出境。

（2）中国游客出境

中国游客出境也须向我口岸边防检查站交验有效护照和前注国家或地区的签证（赴香港、澳门地区须提交《注来港澳通行证》和签注，赴台湾地区提交《大陆居民注来台湾通行证》和签注）。

中国游客出境前，若携带单价超过 5,000 元的手表、相机、摄像机等贵重物品，需在托运行李前向海关申报，填写《出境旅客行李物品申报单》。

3. 中国海关的有关规定

根据《中华人民共和国海关法》和《中华人民共和国海关对进出境旅客行李物品监管办法》的规定，进出境的旅客行李物品必须通过设有海关的地点进境或出境，接受海关监管。旅客应按规定向海关申报。

旅客进出境携有需向海关申报的物品，应在申报台前向海关递交《中华人民共和国海关进出境旅客行李物品申报单》或海关规定的申报单证，按规定如实申报其行李物品，报请海关办理物品进境或出境手续。在实施双通道制的海关现场，上述旅客应选择"申报"通道（亦称"红色通道"）通关；携带无须向海关申报的物品的旅客即可选择"无申报"通道（亦称"绿色通道"通关）。

部分限制进出境物品：

① 烟、酒

② 旅行自用物品

非居民旅客及持有前注国家或地区再入境签证的居民旅客携带旅行自用物品：照相机、便携式收录音机、小型摄影机、手提式摄录机、手提式文字处理机每种一件。超出范围的或单价超过 5,000 元的需向海关如实申报，并办理有关手续。经海关放行的旅行自用物品，旅客应在回程时复带出境。

③ 金、银及其制品

旅客携带金、银及其制品入境应以自用合理数量为限，其中超过 50 克的应填写申报单证，向海关申报；复带出境时，海关凭本次进境申报的数量核放。

携带或托运出境在中国境内购买的金、银及其制品（包括镶嵌饰品、器皿等新工艺品），海关验凭中国人民银行制发的"特种发票"放行。

模块八 特殊问题处理

Module 8 Handling Special Events

任务描述 Task Description

　　特殊问题,是指在导游带团过程中,遇到的一些突发性的问题与事故。作为一名合格的导游,不仅要具备独立工作能力、组织协调能力,还应该具有处理和解决常见问题和特殊问题的应变能力。

Special events refer to unexpected problems or accidents during the tour. A qualified tour guide should not only have the ability of working independently, organizing things and coordinating with others, but also have the ability to solve common problems and deal with special events.

任务目标 Learning Objectives

　　1. 了解旅游过程中可能出现的特殊问题及解决方法,能用英语进行这方面的交流。

Know about different kinds of problems and special events arising in the tour, and learn how to talk about them in English.

　　2. 掌握处理特殊问题中的英文写作技能。

Develop English writing ability in dealing with special events.

　　3. 练习处理旅游中的交通事故、投诉及游客的其他特殊情况。

Practice handling traffic accidents, complaints from the tourists and other special happenings or problems.

特殊问题 Special Events

1. 旅游中出现的交通事故
traffic accidents in tour
2. 游客的特殊要求
special requests of tourists
3. 游客的投诉
complaints made by tourists
4. 游客生病、受伤
tourists' getting sick or hurt
5. 游客财物丢失
tourists' losing their belongings

小贴士 Tips

旅游投诉

1. 如何提防旅游业名不副实的欺诈行为？

最常见的旅游业欺诈行为发生在团体旅游的全包价旅游中。全包价旅游指游客支付的旅游费用包括所有服务项目：食、住、行、游、娱等的旅游。一些违规旅行社以全包价旅游招揽游客，但游客实际享受的是半包价旅游，如旅行社只包住、行、游览的费用，而其他方面让游客自理。有些所谓的"全包旅游"还要游客自付游览门票，自付某一顿饭钱，或是自付机场建设费，等等。为防止这种欺诈行为，游客要先与旅游公司签好合同，或要求旅游公司在出行前写明食宿标准和每天的具体旅游安排，以便出现欺诈行为后到有关部门投诉。

2. 怎样实施旅游投诉？

2010 年 7 月 1 日起施行的由国家旅游局颁布的《旅游投诉处理办法》指出，"为了维护旅游者和旅游经营者的合法权益，依法公正处理旅游投诉"。投诉是旅游活动中时有发生的一种现象。当游客或旅游经营者认为自己的合法权益受到侵害时，可以用书面或口头形式向旅游管理部门或当地旅游局提出投诉。游客投诉时应有相关证据，比如与旅行社签订的合同等。

（http://www.chuguo.cn/travel/204985.xhtml.）

课堂实训　In-class Practice

实训项目1　Task 1

写作实训：事故报告

Writing：Accident Report

实训要求：澳大利亚AU0606旅游团抵达中山陵停车场。一名游客下车时不慎摔伤左脚踝关节。导游王小姐叫来了救护车把伤者送到了医院,伤者在医院得到了及时的治疗,目前情况稳定。王小姐现需就交通事故情况撰写一份事故报告。

Directions：The Australian tour group AU0606 arrived at the parking lot at Dr. Sun Yat-sen's Mausoleum. When getting off the coach, one of the tourists slipped and her left ankle got injured. Miss Wang, the tour guide called for an ambulance and the injured was sent to the hospital, received timely treatment and is now in a stable condition. Miss Wang is required to write an accident report to the department.

英文事故报告一般包括以下几个部分:

English accident report usually consists of the following parts:

1. 报告接收者(To)

2. 报告提交者(From)

3. 报告日期(Date)

4. 报告主题(Subject)

5. 背景介绍(Background)

6. 报告内容(Particulars):(1)事故经过(Happening);(2)采取的措施(Measures taken)

7. 结果和建议(Settlement and suggestions)

示例　Model

To：Department Officer

From：Miss Wang, Tour Guide, NJ ＊＊ Travel Agency

Date：June 12, 2016

Subject：One person injured

One tourist of Group AU0606, consisting of 18 tourists, got injured on the tour to Dr. Sun Yat-sen's Mausoleum on June 12, 2016. The following is a brief account of the accident.

Our group arrived at Dr. Sun Yat-sen's Mausoleum at 9 a. m. on June 12, 2016. After the coach stopped at the parking lot, the tourists got off the bus. Ms. Kewell Walker slipped and her left ankle got injured. Lu Fan, the national guide, helped her sit in a safe place and Wang Yun, the tour guide immediately called 120 for an ambulance. The ambulance came in 10 minutes and Ms. Walker was sent to the Emergency Department of Nanjing Hospital and received timely treatment. Now she is back and in a stable condition.

We feel sorry for what happened. In the future, we will see to it that more safety measures are taken to ensure the tourists' safety.

（栾丽君：《新航标职业英语·英语写作实训教程（旅游专业）》，北京语言大学出版社，2011 年。）

实训项目2　Task 2

情景对话： 处理客人投诉

Dialogue： Dealing with the Complaints of the Tourists

实训要求： 卡特夫人对在南京的旅游提出了投诉，投诉事由：旅行社违反承诺更换导游；上一个导游擅自变换游览线路，并威胁甩客。上海的导游对卡特夫人提出的投诉进行了处理。

Directions： Mrs. Carter has made a complaint about changing guides, which broke the promise by the Travel Agency, and the last guide's forcing to change the scheduled sightseeing route and threatening to leave the tourists alone during her travel in Nanjing, and the tour guide in Shanghai is handling her complaint.

示例　Model

（G：tour guide　C：Mrs. Carter）

G：Good morning. Is there anything I can do for you?

C：Yes. I'm Mrs. Carter. I think I have a complaint to make about our travel in Nanjing.

G：I'm sorry to hear that. What happened?

C：Well, we chose the travel line named "Free Trip" in Nanjing in your travel agency. At first you promised to provide the same tour guide to accompany us for the whole trip. And you promised that it was a fine line with wonderful interesting places. But we found that the tour guide disappeared when we checked in for the flight to Nanjing. After we got off the plane, we were sent to a hotel by another tour guide. Afterwards we knew the guy was a local tour guide in Nanjing. The worst thing was that they changed our tour guides two times in the whole tour.

G: Well, you know, madam, in general, one local guide is responsible for the tasks in one destination. So we usually change local tour guides for different cities.

C: But you didn't tell us in advance. What's more, the last tour guide made a bold change in the arranged route. When we refused to accept it, he became very angry and threatened to leave us alone. At last, we had to give in. So we didn't see those so-called wonderful interesting places. We never expected this sort of thing would happen with a well-run travel agency.

G: Thank you for telling us about it. I'm sorry, madam, there may be some misunderstanding. In general, our tour guide must obey the travel contract. I will look into it and give you a reply as soon as possible. Could you give me your number so that I can reach you?

C: My mobile telephone number is 126 ** 458922.

G: We'll see into it thoroughly. Is there anything else?

C: No, thank you.

G: You are welcome. Sorry for the inconvenience.

小贴士 Tips

踏青旅游安全小常识

随着人们生活水平的提高，开车外出踏青旅游的人明显增多。在享受大自然带给我们快乐的同时，多发的交通事故也给我们敲响了警钟。踏青旅游本是追求美好生活、轻松愉快的美事，可为什么容易引发交通事故呢？其主要原因有：

一是超速行驶。出行时，往往因为没有根据假日时间科学安排行程而造成争分夺秒、超速行驶的现象，从而引发事故。

二是乱停滥放。不少旅游出行的人不遵守车辆停放规定，而是根据自己的喜好随意停放车辆，喜欢在路边赏景，这既影响了交通，又容易造成事故发生。

三是"生手"开车。外出旅游能够使人身心放松，但有些人由于交通安全意识薄弱，借机让平时不怎么开车的"生手"练车，甚至让没有驾驶证的家人开车，这也极易造成事故和不可挽回的后果。

四是酒后开车。一家人出门踏青旅游，有人就放松了对自己的要求和对事故的警惕，认为出门就要玩个痛快，因此，经不住他人的劝让，开怀畅饮，酒后开车，结果造成了惨痛的车祸，害了自己，更害了家人。

五是疲劳开车。驾驶人连续驾驶的安全时间是有限的，有些家庭安排行程不考虑安全因素，盲目行驶过长的路程，使得驾驶人昼夜兼程，导致精神疲惫，很难保证其安全行车。

踏青旅游，勿忘安全；遵法出行，平安回家。希望广大驾车人员从以上分析中受到教育，得到启发，以对自身安全、家庭幸福高度负责的精神，牢牢把握安全行车的主动权，在谨慎驾驶、确保安全的前提下，享受明媚的阳光和美好的视觉盛宴。

课后实训　After-class Practice

实训项目　Task

实用写作：事故报告

Writing：Accident Report

实训要求：南京旅行社地接导游王小姐接待的是一个来自澳大利亚的 18 人旅游团。第二天游览了南京夫子庙，大家正在返回酒店的途中。下午 5 点左右，在距酒店约 2 公里的地方，一辆大巴（牌照为苏 A ** 302）在躲避一辆自行车时突然撞向我们的旅游客车。我们的司机（马乐）猛踩刹车，避免了两车相撞。但是，刹车造成了本旅行团中没有系安全带的两位客人——威尔森小姐和亨特先生——被甩出了座椅而受伤。在旅游团领队的陪同下，他们两人被及时送到了附近的第二人民医院。两位伤者在医院接受了所有必要的检查和治疗。一天后,医院批准他们出院,并出具了医疗检查报告。

Directions: Miss Wang, tour guide of NJ ** Travel Service is the local guide of the Australian tour group of 18 tourists. On the second day of their tour in Nanjing, the group visited the Confucius Temple and was on the way back to the hotel. At about 5: 00 p. m. , 2 km away from the hotel, a bus(苏 A ** 302) suddenly swerved towards our tour coach when it tried to avoid a bike. Our driver, Mr. Ma Le responded by braking suddenly and fortunately escaped the collision. As a consequence of the sudden brake, two tourists of the group, Miss Wilson and Mr. Hunter who didn't fasten their seatbelts, were thrown out of their seats and injured. They were sent to the nearby No. 2 Hospital immediately accompanied by the tour leader. And they received all the necessary examinations and treatment at the hospital. One day after the accident, the hospital was confident to release them and issued a medical check report.

示例 Model

To: Department Officer

From: Miss Wang, Tour Guide, NJ ** Travel Agency

Date: June 14, 2016

Subject: Two persons injured

The Australian tour group arrived in Nanjing on June 11, 2016. On the second day of their tour in Nanjing, the group visited the Confucius Temple according to the itinerary. Unfortunately, a traffic accident happened late in the afternoon on the way back to the hotel.

On the way back to the hotel, at about 5: 00 p. m. , 2 km away from the hotel, a bus(苏 A ** 302) suddenly swerved towards our tour coach when it tried to avoid a bike. Our driver, Mr. Ma Le responded by braking suddenly and fortunately escaped the collision. As a consequence of the sudden brake, two tourists of the group, Miss Wilson and Mr. Hunter who didn't fasten their seatbelts, were thrown out of their seats and injured. They were sent to the nearby No. 2 Hospital immediately accompanied by the tour leader. And they received all the necessary examinations and treatment at the hospital. One day after the accident, the hospital was confident to release them and issued a medical check report.

We feel sorry for what happened and we will see to it that safety measures are strengthened in the future.

语言储备 Words and Expressions

1. 专业术语　Special Terms

flight delay	航班延误
flight cancellation	航班取消
weather forecast	天气预报
tropical storm	热带风暴
typhoon	台风
tornado	龙卷风
flood	水灾
snow storm	暴风雪
traffic jam	交通堵塞
traffic accident	交通事故
fire	火灾
earthquake	地震
lose one's belongings	丢失财物
lose one's way	迷路
physical assault	人身伤害
food poisoning	食物中毒
first aid	急救
incident/accident handling	事故处理
incident/accident investigation	事故调查
incident/accident description	事故过程描述
write a report of the incident /accident	写事故报告
medical treatment	医学治疗
extent of injury	受伤程度
take full responsibility	承担全部责任
have joint responsibility	负有共同责任
compensation	补偿

2. 实用句型　Useful Sentences

(1) This is a written account of the accident.

这是一份事故情况报告。

（2）We are now on the way to the hospital.

我们现在正在前往医院的途中。

（3）Three tourists were slightly injured in the accident.

三名游客在事故中轻微受伤。

（4）The injured were given timely treatment in hospital.

受伤者在医院得到了及时治疗。

（5）On the way, the tour group came across a storm, which delayed our sightseeing for about an hour.

途中，旅游团遇上了暴风雨，参观延误了大约一个小时。

（6）We are taking measures to prevent this type of incident/accident from happening again.

我们正在采取措施避免类似事件发生。

（7）The injured have received all the necessary examinations and treatment.

对伤者进行了所有必要的检查和治疗。

（8）We see to it that this sort of things will never happen again.

我们保证将不会再发生此类事件。

▰▱ 知识链接 Related Knowledge

旅游安全管理暂行办法实施细则

第一章　总则

第一条　为贯彻落实《旅游安全管理暂行办法》，特制定本细则。

第二章　安全管理

第二条　旅游安全管理工作实行在国家旅游管理部门的统一领导下，各级旅游行政管理部门分级管理的体制。

第三条　各级旅游行政管理部门依法保护旅游者的人身、财物安全。

第四条　国家旅游行政管理部门安全管理工作的职责是：

（一）制定国家旅游安全管理规章，并组织实施；

（二）会同国家有关部门对旅游安全实行综合治理，协调处理旅游安全事故和其它安全问题；

（三）指导、检查和监督各级旅游行政管理部门和旅游企事业单位的旅游安全管理工作；

（四）负责全国旅游安全管理的宣传、教育工作，组织旅游安全管理人员的培训工作；

（五）协调重大旅游安全事故的处理工作；

（六）负责全国旅游安全管理方面的其它有关事项。

第五条　县级以上（含县级）地方旅游行政管理部门的职责是：

（一）贯彻执行国家旅游安全法规；

（二）制定本地区旅游安全管理的规章制度，并组织实施；

（三）协同工商、公安、卫生等有关部门，对新开业的旅游企事业单位的安全管理机构、规定制度及其消防、卫生防疫等安全设施、设备进行检查，参加开业前的验收工作；

（四）协同公安、卫生、园林等有关部门，开展对旅游安全环境的综合治理工作，防止向旅游者敲诈、勒索、围堵等不法行为的发生；

（五）组织和实施对旅游安全管理人员的宣传、教育和培训工作；

（六）参与旅游安全事故的处理工作；

（七）受理本地区涉及旅游安全问题的投诉；

（八）负责本地区旅游安全管理的其它事项。

第六条　旅行社、旅游饭店、旅游汽车和游船公司、旅游购物商店、旅游娱乐场所和其它经营旅游业务的企事业单位是旅游安全管理工作的基层单位，其安全管理工作的职责是：

（一）设立安全管理机构，配备安全管理人员；

（二）建立安全规章制度，并组织实施；

（三）建立安全管理责任制，将安全管理的责任落实到每个部门、每个岗位、每个职工；

（四）接受当地旅游行政管理部门对旅游安全管理工作的行业管理和检查、监督；

（五）把安全教育、职工培训制度化、经常化，培养职工的安全意识，普及安全常识，提高安全技能，对新招聘的职工，必须经过安全培训，合格后才能上岗；

（六）新开业的旅游企事业单位，在开业前必须向当地旅游行政管理部门申请对安全设施设备、安全管理机构、安全规章制度的检查验收，检查验收不合格者，不得开业；

（七）坚持日常的安全检查工作，重点检查安全规章制度的落实情况和安全管理漏洞，及时消除安全隐患；

（八）对用于接待旅游者的汽车、游船和其它设施，要定期进行维修和保

养,使其始终处于良好的安全技术状况,在运营前进行全面的检查,严禁带故障运行;

(九)对旅游者的行李要有完备的交接手续,明确责任,防止损坏或丢失;

(十)在安排旅游团队的游览活动时,要认真考虑可能影响安全的诸项因素,制定周密的行程计划,并注意避免司机处于过分疲劳状态;

(十一)负责为旅游者投保;

(十二)直接参与处理涉及单位的旅游安全事故,包括事故处理、善后处理及赔偿事项等;

(十三)开展登山、汽车、狩猎、探险等特殊旅游项目时,要事先制定周密的安全保护预案和急救措施,重要团队需按规定报有关部门审批。

第三章 事故处理

第七条 凡涉及旅游者人身、财物安全的事故均为旅游安全事故。

第八条 旅游安全事故分为轻微、一般、重大和特大事故四个等级:

(一)轻微事故是指一次事故造成旅游者轻伤,或经济损失在1万元以下者;

(二)一般事故是指一次事故造成旅游者重伤,或经济损失在1万至10万(含1万)元者;

(三)重大事故是指一次事故造成旅游者死亡或旅游者重伤致残,或经济损失在10万至100万(含10万)元者;

(四)特大事故是指一次事故造成旅游者死亡多名,或经济损失在100万元以上,或性质特别严重,产生重大影响者。

第九条 事故发生后,现场有关人员应立即向本单位和当地旅游行政管理部门报告。

第十条 地方旅游行政管理部门在接到一般、重大、特大安全事故报告后,要尽快向当地人民政府报告,对重大、特大安全事故,要同时向国家旅游行政管理部门报告。

第十一条 一般、重大、特大安全事故发生后,地方旅游行政管理部门和有关旅游企事业单位要积极配合有关方面,组织对旅游者进行紧急救援,并妥善处理善后事宜。

第四章 奖励与惩罚

第十二条 对在旅游安全管理工作中有下列先进事迹之一的单位,由各级旅游行政管理部门进行评比考核,给予表扬和奖励:

(一)旅游安全管理制度健全,预防措施落实,安全教育普及,安全宣传和

培训工作扎实,在防范旅游安全事故方面成绩突出,一年内未发生一般性事故的;

(二)协助事故发生单位进行紧急救助、避免重大损失,成绩突出的;

(三)在旅游安全其它方面做出突出成绩的。

第十三条 对在旅游安全管理工作中有下列先进事迹之一的个人,由各级旅游行政管理部门进行评比考核,给予表扬和奖励:

(一)热爱旅游安全工作,在防范和杜绝本单位发生安全事故方面成绩突出的;

(二)见义勇为,救助旅游者,或保护旅游者财物安全不受重大损失的;

(三)及时发现事故隐患,避免重大事故发生的;

(四)在旅游安全其它方面做出突出成绩的。

第十四条 对在旅游安全管理工作中有下列情形之一者,由各级旅游行政管理部门检查落实,对当事人或当事单位负责人给予批评或处罚:

(一)严重违反旅游安全法规,发生一般、重大、特大安全事故者;

(二)对可能引发安全事故的隐患,长期不能发现和消除,导致重大、特大安全事故发生者;

(三)旅游安全设施、设备不符合标准和技术要求,长期无人负责,不予整改者;

(四)旅游安全管理工作混乱,造成恶劣影响者。

第五章 附则

第十五条 本实施细则由国家旅游局负责解释。

第十六条 本实施细则自1994年3月1日起施行。

附录一　重点旅游城市英文简介

Appendix 1　Brief Introduction of Key Tourism Cities

Beijing

Beijing, the capital of China, is one of the world's famous historic and cultural cities. As a city with more than 3,000 years of recorded history, Beijing served as the capital of five dynasties, including Liao, Jin, Yuan, Ming and Qing, for about 800 years. Beijing is China's political, economic, cultural and educational center and a hub for international trade and communication as well.

In the city, cultural heritage sites and scenic spots can be found everywhere. The Forbidden City, the Great Wall, the Zhoukoudian Site, the Temple of Heaven, the Summer Palace, and the Ming Tombs, have all been put on the list of the UNESCO World Heritage Sites. The Forbidden City is the largest royal palace in the world and the Great Wall the only man-made construction that could be seen in the space. The Temple of Heaven is regarded as the soul of Chinese ancient architecture and the Summer Palace is a classic composition of ancient royal gardens.

The Temple of Heaven

As the largest city central square in the world, the solemn and majestic

Tian'anmen Square is not only the symbol of Beijing but also that of China. The square is surrounded by a variety of significant edifices: the National Museum of China, the Great Hall of the People, Chairman Mao's Memorial Hall, the Monument to People's Heroes, Tian'anmen Gate, Qianmen(Front Gate) and so on.

Other representatives for Beijing are Hutongs(alleys) and square courtyards. Although they are vanishing and being replaced by modern blocks, the government does preserve and restore some of the typical ones in places like Shichahai and Nanchizi, and visitors may go to see or go around them.

The Summer Palace

"Beijing Flavor", Beijing cuisine and other foods, is full of local flavors and has become an important attraction for visitors from home and abroad. Beijing Roast Duck is of course the most well-known. Manhan Quanxi (Manchu-Han Chinese Full Banquet), a traditional banquet originally intended for ethnic-Manchu emperors of the Qing Dynasty, remains very prestigious, expensive and popular. Fuling Jiabing is a famous Beijing

Beijing Roast Duck

snack food, a pancake resembling a flat disk with filling made from Fuling, a traditional Chinese medicine which does good to health.

Beijing develops its general commercial layout and business facilities according to the requirements for an international modern city. It has constructed several large-scale commercial and cultural centers like Wangfujing and Xidan with good shopping environment and cultural atmosphere. Beijing has the most comprehensive urban traffic system in China, with more than 700 bus lines, 15 rail transit lines and over 67,000 taxis.

主要风景名胜	**Attractions in Beijing**
天安门广场	Tian'anmen Square
故宫	The Palace Museum (The Forbidden City)
颐和园	The Summer Palace
天坛	The Temple of Heaven
圆明园	Yuanming Yuan (The Old Summer Palace)
长城	The Great Wall
十三陵	The Ming Tombs
香山公园	Xiangshan Park
中山公园	Zhongshan Park
北海公园	Beihai Park
主要特色产品	**Local Products and Produce of Beijing**
北京烤鸭	Beijing Roast Duck
茯苓夹饼	Fuling Jiabing
北京酥糖	Beijing Crunchy Candy
北京果脯	Beijing Preserved Fruit
六必居酱菜	Lubiju Pickles
景泰蓝	Cloisonne Enamel
牙雕	Ivory Carving
毛猴	Maohou
漆雕	Carved Lacquerware
吹糖人	Blowing Sugar
捏面人	Dough Figurine

Xi'an

Xi'an, which was called Chang'an in ancient times, is the capital city of Shaanxi Province. It is located in the middle of the Guanzhong Plain. As one of the top seven regional central cities of China, Xi'an is also a center of innovation and technology in Asia and functions as the

The Big Wild Goose Pagoda

manufacturing base of large aircraft in China. The city has become the largest central city along the Chinese section of the new Eurasia Land Bridge across the Yellow River basin. Since there are many key institutions of higher learning in the city, Xi'an is one of the most powerful cities in China in the areas of science and technology. Xi'an is unique, with the largest and most important bases of scientific research, higher education, national defense technology and hi-tech industries in middle and western China. It is also the financial and transport center in the area. In the Development Program of the Guanzhong-Tianshui Economic Zone promulgated by the central government, Xi'an has been regarded as the third "international metropolis" of China following Beijing and Shanghai.

Shaanbei Paper-cut

A famous historic and cultural city in China, Xi'an is ranked first among the ancient capitals in China as the city has the largest number of the dynasties taking it as their capital. Its influence has been very great. Xi'an is the cradle of the Chinese nationality, the birthplace of Chinese civilization and the representative of Chinese culture. In

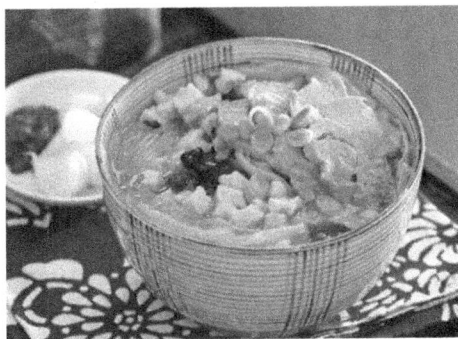

Pita Bread Soaked in lamb Soup

the remote antiquity of China, "Lantian Ape Man" lived in the region of Xi'an; in the Neolithic Period, "Banpo Villagers" settled here to set up their tribes; in the 11th century BC, King Wen of the Zhou Dynasty established the two capitals of Feng and Gao at the banks of the Fenghe River which initiated the brilliant history of Xi'an as a thousand-year capital of China. The city was first established more than 3,100 years ago and it has been taken as a capital for 1,129 years for 13 dynasties, including Western Zhou, Qin, Western Han, Xin, Eastern Han, Western Jin, Former Zhou, Former Qin, Later Qin, Western Wei, Northern Zhou, Sui and Tang. Xi'an is on the list of Top Four Ancient Capitals of the world, in the company of Athens, Rome and Cairo. The city once functioned as the political, economic and cultural center of China and as the starting point of the renowned "Silk Road". Xi'an is one of China's earliest cities opened to the outside world. In the city, there is one of the World Eight Wonders: Qin Shi Huang Terracotta Warriors and Horses, which reveals the foundation of the culture and history of Xi'an. Thanks to its long history and rich culture, the city is reputed to be the natural history museum. There are various cultural relics and historical sites in Xi'an; their total number and values rank first among the cities of China. Some of the cultural relics are unique in China and quite rare in the world.

主要风景名胜	**Attractions in Xi'an**
大雁塔	The Big Wild Goose Pagoda
小雁塔	The Small Wild Goose Pagoda

秦始皇兵马俑博物馆	The Museum of Qin Shi Huang Terracotta Warriors and Horses
秦始皇陵	The Tomb of Emperor Qin Shi Huang
鼓楼	The Drum Tower
钟楼	The Bell Tower
西安城墙	Xi'an City Wall
华清池	Huaqing Hot Spring
法门寺	The Famen Temple
黄河壶口瀑布	The Hukou Waterfall of the Yellow River
大唐芙蓉园	The Tang Paradise

主要特色产品	**Local Products and Produce of Xi'an**
羊肉泡馍	Pita Bread Soaked in Lamb Soup
凉皮	Cold Rice Noodles
肉夹馍	Rougamo
韭菜盒子	Fried Leek Dumplings
刀削面	Sliced Noodles
蓝田玉	Lantian Jade
凤翔彩绘泥塑	Fengxiang Colored Clay Sculpture
唐三彩	Tricolor-glazed Pottery of the Tang Dynasty
碑林拓片	Stele Rubbings
陕北剪纸	Shaanbei Paper-cut
冬青木烙花筷	Holly Pyrographic Chopsticks

Nanjing

As the capital of Jiangsu Province, Nanjing is a prominent city with time-honored history and profound culture. Located in the lower Yangtze River drainage basin and Yangtze River Delta economic zone, Nanjing has always been one of China's most important cities. It served as the capital of China during several historical periods and dynasties such as Eastern Wu, Eastern Jin, Song, Qi, Liang, Chen, Southern Tang, Ming, Taiping Heavenly Kingdom and Republic of China. Therefore, Nanjing enjoys the reputation of "the Ancient Capital of Six Dynasties and the Metropolis of Ten Dynasties". Nanjing, together with Beijing, Luoyang, and Xi'an(Chang'an), is listed as one of "the Four Great Ancient Capitals of China".

Nanjing was one of the earliest established cities in the southern China area. According to the legend, Fu Chai, the Lord of the State of Wu, founded the first city Yecheng in today's Nanjing area in 495 BC. Later in 473 BC, the State of Yue conquered Wu and constructed the city of Yuecheng on the outskirts of the present-day Zhonghua Gate. In 333 BC, after eliminating the State of Yue, the State of Chu built Jinling Yi in the northwestern part of the present-day Nanjing. Under the Qin and the Han dynasties, it was called Moling. Since then, the city has experienced destruction and renewal many times. Nanjing first became a capital in the year of 229, where Sun Quan of the Wu Kingdom during the Three Kingdoms Period relocated its capital to Jianye, a city he had extended on the basis of Jinling Yi in 211. Then it was named as Jiankang. The city's status as a hub of the textile industry had not been consolidated until the Yuan Dynasty.

Dr. Sun Yat-sen's Mausoleum

In 1368, the first emperor of the Ming Dynasty Zhu Yuanzhang (the Hongwu Emperor) rebuilt the city and made it the capital of China. He constructed what was the longest city wall at that time. It took 200,000 laborers 21 years to finish the project. The present-day city wall of Nanjing was mainly built during that time, and it is the longest

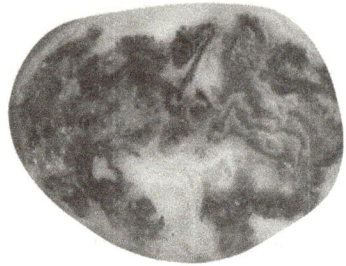

Nanjing Yuhua Stone

surviving city wall in the world. It is believed that Nanjing was the largest city worldwide from 1358 to 1425 with a population of 487,000 in 1400. As the center of the empire, the early-Ming Nanjing was the home of Admiral Zheng He. He had sailed across the Pacific Ocean and the Indian Ocean 7 times in his life, which turned out to be a significant milestone in Chinese history.

Today, with a long cultural tradition and strong support from the local educational institutions, Nanjing is commonly viewed, in China as a "city of culture" and one of the more pleasant cities to live in. For tourists, Nanjing is one of China's most attractive cities. It has a balanced layout between traditional and modern architectural designs. Many broad boulevards are well shaded from the summer heat by tall plane trees. In the center of the city, the beautiful and peaceful Xuanwu Lake with its forested islands smooths out the tough and harsh of a commercial and transportation hub. Meanwhile, there are a lot of places of interests and scenic spots worth visiting, Dr. Sun Yat-sen's Mausoleum, the Ming Tomb, the Confucius Temple along the Qinhuai River and so on.

Plum blossom is the city flower of Nanjing. Every year since 1996, Nanjing Municipal Government holds Nanjing International Plum Blossom Festival at Plum Blossom Hill in Dr. Sun Yatsen's Mausoleum Scenic Area. It attracts millions of visitors every year when many blossom-themed activities are held from February to March. The festival has become a state-level tourism event renowned both at home and abroad.

Due to its abundant produce resources and long food tradition, Nanjing has its unique Huaiyang cuisine and Qinhuai flavor snacks. Nanjing's duck dishes, with a history of 1,400 years, are well-known throughout the country. Besides the salted duck, there are pressed salted duck, Jinling roast duck, Jinling sauced duck, and fragrant crisp duck etc. Also, the dishes made from local ingredients like "eight water delicacies"(edible stems or fruits of water growing plants) and "eight land delicacies"(edible wild vegetables) are very popular.

Nanjing's nightlife used to be mostly centered around the Confucius Temple area along the Qinhuai River, where night markets and restaurants thrived. Boating at night in the river was a main attraction of the city. In the past 20 years, several commercial streets (plazas) have been developed in other areas in Nanjing, so the nightlife has

Nanjing Cloud Brocade(Yunjin)

become decentralized. There are shopping malls opening late in the Xinjiekou and Hunan Road CBD. The well-established "Nanjing 1912" district hosts a wide variety of pastime facilities ranging from traditional restaurants, western pubs to dance clubs. However, local traditions along the Qinhuai River never fail. Since 1985 Qinhuai Lantern Festival has been successfully held at Qinhuai Scenic Zone, which becomes an important component of Qinhuai culture and a famous traditional festival of Nanjing. Each year from January to February, great numbers of citizens and tourists both from home and abroad go to the lantern shows of the Festival. Nanjing charms people with its brilliant tradition and vital fashion.

主要风景名胜	**Attractions in Nanjing**
中山陵	Dr. Sun Yat-sen's Mausoleum
明孝陵	The Ming Tomb
夫子庙	The Confucius Temple
秦淮河风光带	The Qinhuai River Scenic Zone
玄武湖	The Xuanwu Lake
瞻园	Zhanyuan Garden
总统府	The Presidential Palace
栖霞山	Qixia Mountain

汤山温泉	Tangshan Hot Spring

主要特色产品   **Local Products and Produce of Nanjing**

南京盐水鸭	Nanjing Salted Duck
南京云锦	Nanjing Cloud Brocade(Yunjin)
南京雨花石	Nanjing Yuhua Stone
南京雨花茶	Nanjing Yuhua Tea
秦淮八绝	Eight Unique Snacks of Qinhuai

Hangzhou

Hangzhou, the capital city of Zhejiang Province, lies on the lower reaches of Qiantang River, about 180 kilometers southeast of Shanghai, and is one of the modern and prosperous cities in China. It covers a total area of 16,596 square kilometers with a population of 6.31 million. As the political, economic and cultural center of Zhejiang, Hangzhou attracts millions of visitors from home and abroad every year for its natural beauty, historical and cultural heritage.

The West Lake

As early as 5,300 years ago, there were human beings living and proliferating in the area of Hangzhou. "Liangzhu Culture", named after Liangzhu Town, Hangzhou City, where it was first discovered, is an important part of the Chinese ancient culture in the Yangtze

Dongpo Pork

River Delta. Archeological findings in Liangzhu Town indicate that a primitive tribal village once prospered on this fertile land by hunting, cultivating and fishing. Since prefecture and county were set up here in the Qin and the Han dynasties, Hangzhou has enjoyed a history of over 2,200 years. It became prosperous and flourishing in the Tang Dynasty. It was the capital of the Wu and Yue States in the 10th century during the Five Dynasties period. It had its political heyday in the Southern Song Dynasty when it served as the capital of China. Hangzhou witnessed a commercial boom in the Ming Dynasty and the Qing Dynasty, which has lasted to the present. Together with Beijing, Xi'an, Luoyang, Kaifeng, Anyang and

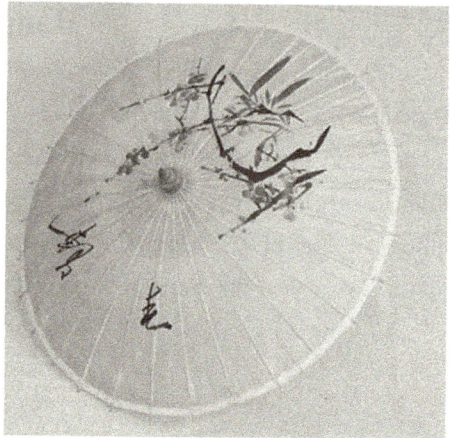

West Lake Silk Umbrella

Nanjing, Hangzhou is known as one of the seven ancient capital cities in Chinese history.

Since ancient times, Hangzhou has been reputed for its production of silk and tea for trade. Here, visitors can find Longjing tea, which is considered one of the best teas in China, exquisite silk brocades, as well as unique handicrafts and artistic pieces. There are several major shopping areas spread all over the city, giving people both traditional and modern shopping experience.

In thousands of years of rich and distinctive history, Hangzhou has passed down, from generation to generation, a unique and unrivaled tradition. Today, in modern Hangzhou, there are a multitude of diverse traditional activities popularized in the folk community which are highly valued and also practiced by local people. Highly romanticized with folklore, this romantic and poetic area is noted for its stories of unrequited love and tragedy, made famous by the love stories of Lady White Snake and Butterfly Lovers, and the legendary stories of Monk Ji Gong. These stories help make Hangzhou what it is today, a city infused with ancient and unforgettable traditions.

主要风景名胜	**Attractions in Hangzhou**
西湖	The West Lake
灵隐寺	Lingyin Temple
雷峰塔	Leifeng Pagoda

宋城	The Song Dynasty Town
千岛湖	The Thousand-Island Lake
西溪湿地	Xixi National Wetland Park
虎跑泉	The Tiger Spring
万松书院	Wansong Academy (Myriad Pine Academy)
六和塔	The Pagoda of Six Harmonies
云栖竹径	The Bamboo-Lined Path at Yunqi
浙西大明山风景区	West Zhejiang's Daming Mountain Scenic Area
杭州极地海洋公园	Hangzhou Polar Ocean Park

主要特色产品	**Local Products and Produce of Hangzhou**
杭州丝绸	Hangzhou Silk
西湖绸伞	West Lake Silk Umbrella
张小泉剪刀	Zhang Xiaoquan Scissors
王星记扇子	Wangxingji Fans
西湖龙井	West Lake Longjing Tea
西湖藕粉	West Lake Lotus Root Powder
西湖醋鱼	West Lake Fish in Vinegar Sauce
龙井虾仁	Fried Shelled Shrimps with Longjing Tea
东坡肉	Dongpo Pork

Suzhou

Suzhou, located in the middle of the Yangtze River Delta, south of Jiangsu Province, covers an area of 8,848 square kilometers. Crisscrossed by rivers, streams and lakes, which make up 42.5% of the city's area, Suzhou is known to the world as the "Venice in the Orient".

Suzhou lies in the temperate zone of a subtropical monsoon climate. Featuring distinctive four seasons, it enjoys a warm weather with ample rainfalls. Camphor tree is its city tree and osmanthus flower is its city flower. Camphor trees line along the streets and osmanthus trees grow in gardens and courtyards, which add to the green and fragrance of the charming city.

The Tiger Hill

The population of Suzhou totaled around 5.99 million with an increase rate of 0.27% up to the end of 2005. The main produces here are rice, cotton, rapeseeds, aromatic non-glutinous rice, purplish glutinous rice and white garlic of Taicang. Taihu Lake whitebait, water shield,

Suzhou Embroidery

pearls and crabs from the Yangcheng Lake and the Taihu Lake here are renowned far and wide.

People say "In the heaven, there's the paradise and on the earth there are Suzhou and Hangzhou". Suzhou is really a "No. 1 area of prosperity and affluence in the world". It is also known as "the city of gardens" to the world. The Humble Administrator's Garden in Suzhou is the largest private garden in the country. It covers a total area of over 14 hectares and now the part opened to visitors takes up only a bit over 5 hectares. The four famous gardens in Suzhou are Canglang Garden of the Song Dynasty, the Garden of Lion Groves, the Humble Administrator's Garden of the Ming and the Lingering Garden left over from the Qing Dynasty.

Neosalanx Taihuensis Soup

As one of the major 10 tourist attractions in China, the gardens of Suzhou attract hundreds and thousands of tourists from home and abroad every year. In addition, Suzhou is also renowned as a "hometown of paintings and writings", a "township of silk-goods" and a "marketplace of arts and crafts".

主要风景名胜	**Attractions in Suzhou**
拙政园	The Humble Administrator's Garden
狮子林	The Lion Forest Garden
沧浪亭	Canglang Pavilion
网师园	The Master-of-Nets Garden
留园	The Lingering Garden
虎丘	The Tiger Hill
艺圃	The Garden of Cultivation
怡园	The Garden of Pleasance
耦园	The Couple's Retreat Garden

主要特色产品	**Local Products and Produce of Suzhou**
苏绣	Suzhou Embroidery
阳澄湖大闸蟹	Yangcheng Lake Hairy Crabs
苏式糕点	Suzhou Pastry
叫花鸡	Beggar's Chicken
苏州缂丝	Kesi Arts in Suzhou
太湖银鱼	Neosalanx Taihuensis
八珍糕	Eight Precious Pudding

Xiamen

Xiamen, a big city of Fujian Province, is located on the southeast coast of China. It has been one of the major seaports since ancient times. Xiamen is a tourist city famous for its attractive seascape. "Xiamen" means "gate of China". It is also called the Egret Island. Hundreds of thousands of egrets inhabit Xiamen because of its beautiful natural scenery, fresh air and good environment.

Lacquer Thread Sculpture

Xiamen has a subtropical climate. It has a mild temperature with abundant rainfalls. The average annual temperature is around 21℃. Winter in Xiamen is not harsh while summer is free from extreme heat. It is good for travelling throughout the year, of which the best tourism season is from April to November.

It covers a total area of about 1,573 square kilometers, with a total population of 6.5 million. It is one of the earliest special economic zones in China. For the purpose of administration, Xiamen is divided into six districts nowadays: Siming, Huli, Jimei, Haicang, Tong'an and Xiang'an.

The Sunlight Rock

Xiamen is an old city with more than 3,000 years of recorded history. The first administrative system was established in Song Dynasty. In the last 1,000 years, it has changed its name several times. In 1993, it was renamed "Xiamen City".

Xiamen is an ideal tourist destination with abundant tourist attractions such as mountains, temples, islands, and waters, etc., providing us with a full sightseeing schedule. The renowned Gulangyu Island, Nanputuo Temple, Wanshiyan and the amazing sceneries of many beautiful small islands are highly recommended.

Maci(Sticky and Sweet cake)

Xiamen enjoys convenient transportation with a most comprehensive urban traffic system. The accommodation in Xiamen is also convenient. There are many star rated hotels good for tourists. Xiamen has plenty of special local products and produce to be added to your shopping list, including various kinds of teas, fruits like sugarcanes, olives and longans as well as sea food such as fish, prawns, crabs, abalones and lancelets.

（李冬梅：《模拟导游》，厦门大学出版社，2011 年。）

主要风景名胜	Attractions in Xiamen
鹭岛	The Egret Island
胡里山炮台	The Hulishan Fortress
嘉禾屿	Jiaheyu (The Golden Harvest Island)
中左所	Zhongzuosuo (The Middle and Left Offices)
南普陀	The Nanputuo Temple
日光岩	The Sunlight Rock
菽庄花园	The Shuzhuang Garden
藏海园	The Garden of Hiding the Sea (Canghaiyuan)
补山园	The Garden of Making-Up Hills (Bushanyuan)

主要特色产品	**Local Products and Produce of Xiamen**
漆线雕	Lacquer Thread Sculpture
柴烧铁观音	Firewood Tieguanyin
香菇肉酱	Xianggu Mushroom Sauce
麻糍	Maci(Sticky and Sweet Cake)
厦门海蛎煎	Xiamen Fried Oyster
花生酥	Peanut Crisp
龙眼	Longan

Guilin

The scenery of Guilin has been called the finest in the world. Situated in the northeast of Guangxi Zhuang Autonomous Region, Guilin enjoys a mild climate with sufficient rainfall. Its yearly average temperature is about 19℃, while August has an average temperature of 28℃ and February 8℃.

The Lijiang River

Guilin at one time was a vast sea until about one hundred and ninety million years ago, when the whole area rose and became land owing to the movement of the earth crust. The limestone, weathered and eroded by water, became today's fantastic stone forests, peaks, underground streams and caves, thus giving unique features to Guilin's scenery.

The mountains and hills in Guilin rise abruptly and stand in various stately shapes. These mountains and caves of unique formation, together with the crystal-clear rivers that surround the city, characterize Guilin's scenery and have brought it worldwide fame. The Elephant Trunk Hill, which has the greatest fame, looks like a giant elephant extending its trunk into the river. It is regarded as a symbol of Guilin. Many Guilin products use the Elephant Trunk Hill as their trademark.

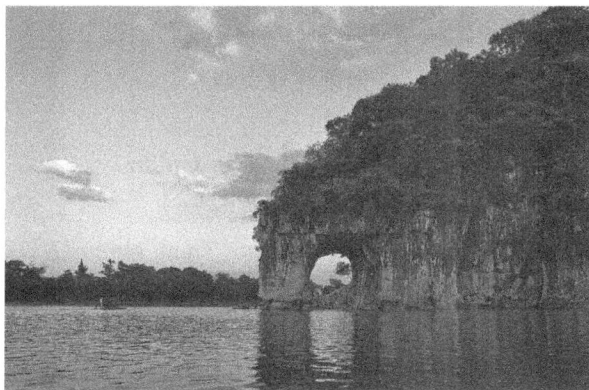

The Elephant Trunk Hill

The Lijiang River from Guilin to Yangshuo is its most beautiful part, with a length of 83 km. Winding her way amidst the mountains and through villages, the Lijiang River adds a great charm to the picture-like landscape of Guilin, where people can see mountains with fantastic peaks,

Yangshuo Fan-drawing

green and clear waters, and artistic fields. The journey, a real treat for tourists, ends at Yangshuo. As the saying goes, "the landscape in Guilin is the best in China, and the landscape in Yangshuo is the best in Guilin". The hills in Yangshuo are close to each other, peaceful and secluded.

Guilin also abounds in historical relics. Stone carvings alone amount to approximately 2,000 pieces. Of all the other scenic spots in the city, Putuo Hill, Crescent Moon Hill and Folded Brocade Hill possess the greatest number of these carvings. The Dragon Refuge Cave, which, as it is lined with stelae, is properly called "Guilin Stele Forest".

Guilin Rice Noodles

As one of the top tourist destinations in China, Guilin will surely continue to attract more visitors from home and abroad.

（许红,张婷:《旅游英语》, 中国林业出版社, 2009 年。）

主要风景名胜	Attractions in Guilin
漓江	The Lijiang River
象鼻山	The Elephant Trunk Hill
叠彩山	Diecai Hill
伏波山	Fubo Hill
芦笛岩	The Reed Flute Cave
七星景区	The Seven Star Scenic Spot

日月双塔	Sun and Moon Pagoda
独秀峰	Solitary Beauty Peak
刘三姐景观园	Liu Sanjie Folk Park
靖江王府	Jingjiang Prince Mansion
主要特色产品	**Local Products and Produce of Guilin**
桂林米粉	Guilin Rice Noodles
桂林腐乳	Guilin Preserved Bean Curd
桂林三花酒	Guilin Sanhua Liquor
桂林辣椒酱	Guilin Chili Sauce
荔浦芋头	Lipu Taro
桂林桂花茶	Guilin Osmanthus Tea
阳朔沙田柚	Yangshuo Shatian Pomelo
阳朔金桔	Yangshuo Kumquat
恭城柿饼	Gongcheng Dried Persimmon
山羊壶	Goat Pot
象山壶	Elephant Hill Pot
山水画瓶系列	Bottle Series of Landscape Paintings
竹木雕刻	Bamboo Carvings
瓷刻	Porcelain Carvings
阳朔画扇	Yangshuo Fan-drawing
壮锦	Zhuang Brocade

附录二　著名旅游景点英文简介

Appendix 2　Brief Introduction of Famous Scenic Spots

The Palace Museum（The Forbidden City）

The Palace Museum, was the imperial palace of the Ming (1368—1644) and the Qing(1644—1912) dynasties. It is better known in the West as the Forbidden City, because in the old days, it was forbidden to ordinary people. The palace is made up of two parts: the outer court and the inner court. The outer court was used by the emperor to handle official affairs (issue decrees, receive officials and foreign visitors, perform ceremonies, behead criminals, etc.). The inner court was the residential quarter, where the emperor, empresses and concubines lived. The whole palace covers more than 70 hectares.

The Forbidden City

Let's take a look at part of the outer palace. Wumen (the Meridian Gate) is the main gate of the Forbidden City. It has five openings. The central passage was reserved for the emperor alone. High-ranking civil and military officials went in through the side gate on the east and the imperial family members on the west. The further side gates were for petty officials. Taihe Dian (the Hall of Supreme Harmony) was the hall where the emperor received senior officials and held ceremonies of important occasions (the enthronement of an emperor, the emperor's birthday, the New Year's Day, the Spring Festival, the announcement of the winners of imperial examinations, the issuing of imperial decrees, the declaration of war, and the like). Zhonghe Dian (the Hall of Central Harmony) was where the emperor took a rest on his way to the Hall of Supreme Harmony and met his cabinet members and officials of the Ministry of Rites. Baohe Dian (the Hall of Preserving Harmony) was a place in which the emperor held the palace examinations for scholars pursuing literary degrees and for his dynasty selecting senior officials. For the examinees, passing the exam meant a guaranteed high position and great credit to the family.

Now we are at the inner palace and let's see some of the spots. Qianqing Gong (the Palace of Heavenly Purity) lies in the foremost place of the Inner Court. In this palace, emperors like Shunzhi and Kangxi (the Qing Dynasty) lived and handled state affairs, reading reports, dispatching and calling in officials and receiving foreign ambassadors. Jiaotai Dian (the Hall of Union and Peace) was a hall where the empresses were conferred honorable titles and held their birthday celebrations. To the east is a water clock made in 1745. Water clocks had been used for quite a long time before the mechanical clock was introduced to China. To the west is the chiming clock made in 1789. Kunning Gong (the Palace of Earthly Tranquility) served as the living quarters for empresses in the Ming Dynasty. In the Qing Dynasty, the palace was converted into the place for sacrifices to the God of the Kitchen. The Eastern Warmth Room was the wedding chamber for the emperors Kangxi, Tongzhi, and Guangxu and their wedding ceremonies were held here. In the rear of the Inner Court, there is the Imperial Garden, where the imperial family could enjoy their leisure time.

There are too many things to be seen. Among them the Clock and Watch Exhibition Hall is a popular attraction for tourists from home and abroad to see how the imperial families and other aristocrats of the Ming and the Qing dynasties lived luxuriously. And the Treasure Hall is another attraction, where there are more than 440 cultural relics on display.

Qin Shi Huang Terracotta
Warriors and Horses

The Terracotta Warriors and Horses are the most significant archeological excavations of the 20th century. The site is around 1.5 kilometers east of Emperor Qin Shi Huang's Mausoleum, Lintong County, Shaanxi Province. It is a sight not to be missed by any visitor to China.

Upon ascending the throne at the age of 13 (in 246 BC), Qin Shi Huang, later the first Emperor of all China, had work begun on his mausoleum. It took 11 years to finish. It is speculated that many buried treasures and sacrificial objects had accompanied the emperor in his after life. A group of peasants uncovered some pottery while digging for a well nearby the royal tomb in 1974. It caught the attraction of archeologists immediately. They came to Xi'an in droves to study and to extend the digs. They established beyond doubt that these artifacts were associated with the Qin Dynasty (221 – 207 BC).

Qin Shi Huang Terracotta Warriors and Horses

The State Council authorized to build a museum on site in 1975. When completed, people from far and near came to visit it in large numbers. Xi'an and the Museum of Qin Shi Huang Terracotta Warriors and Horses have become a must on all travellers' itinerary.

Life size terracotta figures of warriors and horses arranged in battle formations are the star features at the museum. They are replicas of what the imperial guard should look like in those days of pomp and vigor.

The museum covers an area of 16,300 square meters, divided into three sections: No. 1 Pit, No. 2 Pit and No. 3 Pit respectively. They were tagged in the order of their discoveries. No. 1 Pit is the largest, first opened to the public on China's National Day, 1979. There are columns of soldiers at the front, followed by war chariots at the back.

No. 2 Pit, found in 1976, is 20 meters northeast of No. 1 Pit. It contained over a thousand warriors and 90 chariots of wood. It was unveiled to the public in 1994. Archeologists came upon No. 3 Pit also in 1976, 25 meters northwest of No. 1 Pit. It looked like the command center of the armed forces. It went on display in 1989, with 68 warriors, a war chariot and four horses.

Altogether over 7,000 pottery soldiers, horses, chariots, and even weapons have been unearthed from these pits. Most of them have been restored to their former grandeur.

The Terracotta Warriors and Horses is a sensational archeological find of all times. It has put Xi'an high up on the list of tour attractions for tourists in China. It was listed by UNESCO in 1987 as one of the world cultural heritages.

The Confucius Temple

In the south of Nanjing sits the Confucius Temple on the bank of the Qinhuai River. First built in the Song Dynasty, it was the ritual place for pupils to pay respects and offer sacrifices to Confucius. But gradually, it was renovated and expanded to a place with a group of Ming and Qing style buildings. In 1997, a street of local delicacies, Former Residence of Wang's and Xie's at Wuyi Lane, and Nanjing Oriental Art Gallery were rebuilt or renovated in this area. Now it has become a replica of traditional local life with typical architectures as well as a commercial and tourist site.

Jiangnan Imperial Examination Center

Located to the east of the Confucius Temple is Jiangnan Imperial Examination Center. Built during the Song Dynasty on a grand scale, it was the place for holding imperial exams at provincial level. Chinese emperors began to select officials through imperial exams from the Sui Dynasty in the 7th century. Jiangnan Imperial Examination Center had its heyday in the early Ming Dynasty when Nanjing was the capital of China. Today visitors can see a watchtower where the invigilators watched the students during the examinations, a good number of stone tablets, and 40 cubicles where the students took the examinations in the daytime and slept at night. Sometimes visitors can also see a demonstration of the imperial examination.

The Confucius Temple

Former Residence of Wang's and Xie's at Wuyi(Black Clothes) Lane

The place was the former army garrison of the Wu Kingdom, which dates back to over 1,700 years ago. The soldiers wore black clothes at that time, so it is called Wuyi Lane. In the early East Jin Dynasty, Prime Minister Wang Dao lived here. Later, it became the residence area for Wang's and Xie's(Xie An was also a high-ranking official during the East Jin Dynasty). During the mid-Tang Dynasty, poet Liu Yuxi visited Wuyi Lane and sighed in his famous poem that "The swallows from the residence of Wang's and Xie's are now entering the ordinary people's houses". The poem gives us some idea of the splendor of Wuyi Lane during the East Jin Dynasty. In 1997, the Qinhuai District government renovated Wuyi Lane and Former Residence of Wang's and Xie's. Now, it provides a wonderful place for tourists to learn about the history of Nanjing during the six dynasties(Wu Kingdom, East Jin, Song, Qi, Liang and Chen dynasties, 229AD – 589AD), because in the residence there are many paintings, books and carvings with high historic and artistic value.

Nanjing Oriental Art Gallery

Located on the Qinhuai River in the Confucius Temple Area, Nanjing Oriental Art Gallery is a building made of blue bricks and tiny tiles. Its graceful courtyard, secluded corridors, doors and windows with carvings and lattices reflect the architectural style of the Ming and the Qing dynasties. The art gallery was also called "Qifeng Gallery", since it was built by Zhu Qifeng, who lived in the period of the late Ming and the early Qing dynasties in Anhui Province. The gallery served as a place for the men in Zhu's family to study for the imperial examinations. This typical Anhui style building is the only one well preserved from the Ming and the Qing periods in the Confucius Temple area.

Folk Art Exhibition

Displayed folk crafts here include kites, scented bags, door paintings, batiks, colored string knots, paper-cuts, masks, tree-root carvings, pyrographs, eccentric stones, South China style paintings and calligraphy, rain flower pebbles and woodcarvings. Also, Shadow Play, which has a history of 1,600 years in China, can be seen here, especially acted by Nanjing Shadow Play Troupe.

The West Lake

Bordering hills on three sides and neighboring downtown Hangzhou on one side, the West Lake forms the centerpiece of not only the West Lake Scenic Area, but also Hangzhou. As the saying goes "Up in the heaven, there is a paradise; down on the earth, there are Suzhou and Hangzhou". Since the ancient time, Hangzhou has won the fame because of the West Lake. It is said there are altogether 36 west lakes in China, but the one in Hangzhou is the best both in natural and manmade beauty.

The West Lake

The name "West Lake" is derived from its location as well as one of the four ancient Chinese beauties—Xi Shi. It is said that she lived in about 2,400 years ago during the Spring and Autumn Period. She looked pretty in plain dress or make-up. When Su Dongpo became the governor of Hangzhou during the Song Dynasty, he compared the lake to the ancient beauty in one of his poems. He believed that the West Lake looked beautiful both in sunshine and in rain. So it was named Xizi Lake after Xi Shi.

More than 2,200 years ago, the West Lake used to be a shallow bay at the confluence of the sea and the Qiantang River. Two hills of the Wu and the Baoshi (Precious Stone) look very much like two promontories ranging respectively on the north and the south of the bay. As time went by, it was separated from the sea by the silt carried by the tidal waves of the Qiantang River. In the Sui Dynasty around 1,400 years ago, it was completely separated from the sea. Covering an area of

6.7 square kilometers, the West Lake is elliptic in shape with an average depth of 2 meters. Surrounded on three sides by hills with one facing the city, the lake gets its water from the springs of the mountains, rain and the Qiantang River.

The characteristics of the layout of the lake can be described as "ONE, TWO, THREE, FOUR", ONE lake, the West Lake; TWO pagodas, Baoshu and Leifeng pagodas; THREE causeways, Su, Bai and Yang Gong causeways; and FOUR islands, Three Pools Mirroring the Moon, Mid-lake Islet, Ruangong Islet and the Solitary Hill.

Top Ten Scenes of the West Lake

The beauty and charm of Spring Dawn at Su Causeway, Breeze-ruffled Lotus at Quyuan Garden, Autumn Moon over the Calm Lake and Lingering Snow on the Broken Bridge can be appreciated all year round. Leifeng Pagoda in Evening Glow and Three Pools Mirroring the Moon, as their names suggest, should be visited at sunset or on moonlit nights. Sights not subject to seasons and weather are Orioles Singing in the Willows, Twin Peaks Piercing the Clouds, Evening Bell Ringing at Nanping Hill and Fish Viewing at the Flower Pond.

North of the West Lake

There are nine scenic spots dispersed along the northern bank of the West Lake. They are, from the most famous to the lesser-known, Yue Fei's Temple and Tomb, Precious Stone Hill, Baochu Pagoda, Yellow Dragon Cave, Zhejiang Library, Baopu Taoist Temple, Ge Hill and Purple Cloud Cave. For western friends, the story of Yue Fei, a patriotic military general living in the Southern Song Dynasty, is more appealing than the tomb and the memorial hall set up in his honor. Yellow Dragon Cave, which nestles at the foot of Precious Stone Hill with the Baochu Pagoda on top, radiates with rustic flavor.

West of the West Lake

To the west of the West Lake, attractions like Lingyin Temple, Peak Flying from Afar, Three Temples at Tianzhu, Hangzhou Botanical Garden, Visiting Lingfeng for Spring Plum Blossoms and Jade Spring might beckon those wanting to savor enticing natural scenery and the allure of Buddhism.

South of the West Lake

The south bank of the West Lake is strewn with a network of sights. Among which, Pagoda of Six Harmonies, Song Dynasty Town, Nine Creeks and Eighteen

Gullies, Bamboo-lined Path at Yunqi, West Lake International Golf & Country Club sparkle like super stars.

East of the West Lake

West Lake's east bank features the fewest attractions. If you have time, Phoenix Mosque, Confucian Temple and Hangzhou Steles and Water City Gate Park are places worthy of half a day's exploration.

Two Famous Restaurants

Ever wonder where to enjoy local gourmet food? Here are two time-honored restaurants in the scenic area.

Louwailou Restaurant: The fame of this 160-year-old restaurant can be explained by its superb local flavor dishes and many renowned scholars and poets who helped to romanticize it, such as Lu Xun, Sun Yat-sen and Pan Tianshou.

Zhiweiguan Restaurant: It is famous for a wide selection of Hangzhou-style dishes.

Two Famous Tea Houses

He Tea House: "He" means "harmony" in Chinese. Entering this tea house, you will feel like you have entered a tasteful antique shop. Surrounded by antiques ranging from 100 to 3,000 years old, you can experience the same refined pastime enjoyed by Chinese aristocracy a thousand years ago.

Qingteng Tea House: Offering amazing scenery of the West Lake, it is a good place to relax. The air is relaxing and the food served is delicious.

The Humble Administrator's Garden

Together with the Summer Palace in Beijing and Chengde Mountain Resort in Hebei, the Humble Administrator's Garden and the Lingering Garden in Suzhou are listed as the four famous gardens in China. The Humble Administrator's Garden is the largest garden of classical style in Suzhou. Initially built in the Ming Dynasty it covers an area of 5.195 hectares. It is a representative masterpiece of all private gardens in the south of the Yangtze River area. It is covered in green with buildings of classical style laid out in a picturesque manner. Its water area takes up around three fifth of the total area.

The Humble Administrator's Garden

Wang Xiancheng had the Humble Administrator's Garden built, who was a high-ranking official in the imperial court under the reign of Zhengde (1506—1521) in the Ming Dynasty. Dismissed at the middle of his age, he returned home. To make known his setback on the road of officialdom he resorted to some phrases from a poetic prose *Stay Home at Leisure* by Pan Yue of the Western Jin Dynasty, which read "Watering garden and selling vegetables for daily meals... this is the politics of a humble administrator", and use "Humble Administrator" as the name of his garden, which suggested that he had no intention to squeeze and scramble with others for power on the arena of officialdom and it was alright to return home tending on flowers and grasses or selling vegetables, a humbler's politics. It's a usual way of sarcasm for self-comfort of a statesman politically frustrated.

There are dragon patterns on the structure left over from the Qing Dynasty in the Humble Administrator's Garden. The dragon used to be the symbol of supreme authority for feudal emperors. Normally as a private garden it was not permitted to carve any dragon pattern anywhere in it. But the Humble Adiministrator's Garden had once been used as the mansion of Li Xiucheng, King of Loyalty of the Taiping Heavenly Kingdom, and therefore, it is not unreasonable to see some "clouds and dragons" on the 18 window-eaves with Datura stramonium(a kind of thorny apple) patterns in the Retaining and Listening Pavilion.

Gulang Island

Gulang Island is a popular tourist attraction in Xiamen. We can get to the island by ferry.

The island covers an area of 1.78 square kilometers, boasting its major scenic spots including Sunlight Rock and Shuzhuang Garden. Its surrounding waters makes up the major part of Xiamen Port, with the Jinmen Islands across.

After the Opium War, Gulang Island became an international settlement, and 13 countries set up consulates on it, among which are the UK, the USA, France, Germany, and Japan. From the middle of the 19th century, western music was introduced into the island and many musicians were produced hence. Now, there are over 100 families of musicians, and the island was crowned "Island of Music" in 2002 by the Chinese Musicians Association.

The buildings of the building complex of Gulang Island were mostly built in the colonial era, a remnant of the concession era in Xiamen. The oldest building was built in 1896, and others were built in the 1920s and 1930s. Some are nicely preserved, while others stand in various stages of

Gulang Island

disrepair. Among them there are many people's residences. Ficus microcarpa trees line the alley, giving the area an even older feel.

On the island there is the former Japanese consulate, and the legendary Xiamen Music School.... As we walk around, we'll see the island's concert hall, a modern architecture which conveys the old idea of looking into the future and is at odds with its surroundings. The nearby building with a gold cross on its top isn't a church but rather a nursing home for the elderly. Of course, tourist shops line the streets selling souvenirs more or less like the fair you'd find in any other southern coastal city.

The peak of Gulang Island is 92.68 meters above sea level. The Sunlight Rock is situated at the top of Longtou Hill(Dragon Head Hill) in the central south of the island. Standing on the round terrace and overlooking in distance on the top of it, you will get a panoramic view of the magnificent scenery of the Island and the whole city.

As soon as we enter the scenic area of Sunlight Rock, we will see a smallish Buddhist temple, and we can pray for good luck with some burning incense. Leaving the temple, we will have to walk a long way of stone steps, along which poems are carved in the stones.

A saying goes that Gulang Island is a must for a tourist to Xiamen. But a more preferable saying goes that the Sunlight Rock is a must for a tourist to Gulang Island. Here, standing at the Tianfeng Terrace (Heavenly Wind Terrace), and looking around, we can see the reflection of hills and lines of huge ships with breezes and waves.

Looking down from the rock, we'll find Gulang Island resembles a colorful boat floating and glittering with blue waves, like a bonsai on a jade plate with infinite scenery and a sleeping beauty behind a muslin curtain with fascinating charm.

Coming down the other side of the Sunlight Rock, we'll spot a beach with a small and shallow swimming area with a protective network around, a necessary precaution, as it's near a very busy shipping channel. On a hot day we may cool ourselves by swimming in it.

Shuzhuang Garden was located at Gangzaihou on the island, constructed in 1913, belonging to a man named Shu Zhuang. The garden was named after him. The whole garden is 20,328 square meters, 3,352 square meters of water area and 2,451 square meters of construction area. It is near the ocean, and consists of two parts: Canghai Garden(Garden of Hiding the Sea) and Bushan Garden(Garden of Making-up Hills). After our entry we will confront a wall which hides the ocean as a screen.

There are five scenic spots in Canghai Garden, namely, Meishou Pavilion, Renqiu Pavilion, Zhenshuai Pavilion, Forty-Four Bridge, and Zhangliang Pavilion, with five tourist attractions, which are Yuanshi Mountain House, Twelve Cave, Yiaiwu Cottage, Tingchao Pavilion, and Xiaolan Pavilion.

（李冬梅：《模拟导游》，厦门大学出版社，2011年。）

West Street, Yangshuo

Situated at the center of Yangshuo county town, West Street is the oldest street in Yangshuo with a history of more than 1,400 years. West Street is now the most prosperous district in Yangshuo.

The world-famous West Street is nearly 800 meters (2625 feet) long and 8 meters (26 feet) wide, meandering in an "S" way along its length. Being completely paved with marble, it is a typical example of a southern China street. West Street is also called "foreigners' street" by many Chinese tourists. However, it is a typical "China Town" in a foreigner's eyes. Don't be surprised if you hear English words spoken by elderly Chinese women, for West Street is called "the global village". Besides the local accent of Yangshuo, English has become the language for daily use. West Street is modern and fashionable, nearly every store has bilingual shop signs, and more than 20 stores have been run by foreigners who have settled here.

In West Street, Chinese visitors may think they are in a foreign land, while foreigners come here to search for the ancient civilization of China. However, whether you are Chinese or a foreigner, West Street is a perfect place to take a rest, both physically and mentally. It will drive all your

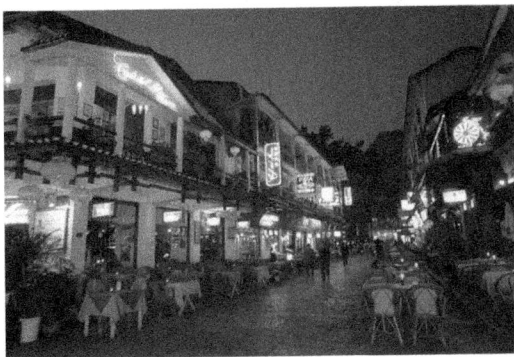

West Street, Yangshuo

pressures and burdens away, and make your life calm. It presents to you different pictures at different times: calm and peaceful in the morning, while trendy and modern in the evening. Traveling to West Street is a wonderful experience when you are close to the landscape, close to your soul, and close to yourself.

Visiting West Street, you will be surrounded by an array of traditional folklore and amazing international elements. Various folk costume stores, traditional craftworks shops, painting and calligraphy stores, backpack shops, cafes, and Chinese Kung Fu academies jostle for attention. You may see a wide variety of items, from embroidered silk cloth, wax-painted weavings to tiny shoes worn by women in old times. In addition, elsewhere on the street you may find bars and cafes, some run by foreigners, decorated with bamboo rafts, fish baskets, wax-painted tablecloths, and so on.

You can treat yourself to the foods of various styles from all over the world in West Street: ciba (a kind of Chinese rice cake), rice noodles of Yangshuo, authentic Italian coffee, banana cake, and Western style food, etc. Well, choose a cafe, ask for a cup of coffee and let the pretty scenery and dulcet music take you to a world of rest and relaxation.

(http://wenku.baidu.com/view/25d91fc6aa00b52acfc7ca1d.html.)

附录三　涉外旅游常用文书
Appendix 3　Tour-related Forms and Writings

01　旅游合同

A Travel Contract

Contract No. _____

BJ ∗∗ Travel Service (hereinafter called Travel Service) and Wayne Carter (hereinafter called Tourist) have on the 10th day of September, 2016 entered into a tour contract under the terms and conditions stated below:

1. Name of tour group

Tourist will join in the 18-day China Discovery Tour (Tour Code _____) organized by Travel Service. Cities to visit include Beijing, Xi'an, Nanjing, and Shanghai. Travel Service shall provide luxury tour group services to Tourist.

2. Time of departure: October 15, 2016

3. Price: US $2,500/P. P.

4. The tour fare includes

(1) Accommodations

Travel Service shall provide Tourist with four-star hotels in the capital cities of provinces in China. Rooms have an attached private bath and air conditioning, as well as a telephone capable of international direct dialing and a television. In smaller towns or rural areas, Travel Service shall provide simple guesthouses. When the hotel listed in the brochure is not available, the same category of hotel will be substituted. Accommodations will be based on double occupancy. If Tourist requests a single room, Tourist shall pay the additional expense.

(2) Meals

Travel Service shall provide daily meals (breakfast, lunch and dinner) in hotels, local restaurants, except for the one or ones specified differently in itinerary and on plane/train. There will be a mix of Western and Chinese meals. Vegetarian food is available upon request.

(3) Admissions/Entrance Fee

Travel Service shall provide with all necessary main entrance fees for the programs or places mentioned in the itinerary.

(4) Transportation

Travel Service shall provide with domestic air/train tickets specified in the itinerary and domestic airport taxes (local construction fee). Travel Service shall provide Tourist with transfer service and coach for overland transportation.

(5) Guide Service

Travel Service shall provide Tourist with the service of a bilingual national guide as well as local guides.

(6) Travel Protection Insurance

Full coverage of Tourist's travel with our protection insurance plan will be provided at no additional cost.

(7) Entertainment

Music and dance performances and other cultural events described in the itineraries will be included in the tour price.

5. The tour fare excludes

(1) Airfare from Tourist's hometown to the gateway city.

(2) Personal expenses.

Tourist shall pay for the single supplement cost for a single room, meals not mentioned in the brochure, extra beverages at meals, food or snacks at times other than regular meal times, excess luggage fees, laundry, postage, telephone, fax or internet/E-mail access charges as well as shopping.

(3) Visa costs.

Tourist shall pay US $50 for obtaining an individual entry visa to China.

(4) Supplementary trips and services not listed in the itinerary.

(5) The extra cost due to the unforeseen events.

6. Terms of Payment

Tourist shall make the full payment upon confirmation of the reservation, 30 days prior to the departure date. The payment shall be remitted to Travel Service in US Dollars. Otherwise Travel Service may cancel the reservation and not return the deposit.

7. Health

(1) Travel Service shall ensure that Tourist is provided with wholesome food and accommodation.

(2) Tourist shall determine whether his physical condition is fit for the tour. Tourist shall be responsible for the cost of any medicines or medical care he may require during the trip for any reason.

(3) Travel Service reserves the right to decline to accept or retain Tourist as a member of the tour, if Tourist's physical condition, mental well-being or behavior interferes with the tour. If Tourist's physical condition, mental well-being or behavior interferes with the operation of the tour, there will be no refund in such cases.

8. Baggage

Baggage is at Tourist's risk throughout. Baggage allowance for transpacific flight is two pieces per person for checked baggage with combined total dimension not exceeding 106 inches provided neither one exceeds 62 inches nor 70 lbs. Baggage allowance in China is restricted to one piece only and to exceed 44 lbs. Carry-on baggage is limited to one piece with combined total dimension not exceeding 45 inches. Tourist will pay the excess baggage charge and insurance.

9. Responsibility

(1) Travel Service acts only in the capacity of an agent for purveyors of transportation, sightseeing and hotel accommodation. All coupons, receipts and tickets issued by Travel Service are subject to the terms and conditions stipulated by the suppliers. Travel Service shall be exempt from any liability for loss or damage to property, injury of persons, accidents, delays, irregularities or other occurrences beyond its control.

(2) Should weather or other unforeseen circumstances cause a delay in transportation before the tour departure, Travel Service may reserve the right to postpone or cancel the tour, and any loss or additional expenses incurred shall be

borne by Tourist. Travel Service reserves the right to rearrange the itinerary or delete activities from the schedule if this becomes necessary due to local conditions. If this happens, the tour prices are subject to change. Any additional expenses incurred shall be charged to Tourist.

(3) Tourist shall strictly abide by the laws and regulations promulgated by the Governments of the countries visited. Tourist shall be responsible for any and all penalties due to any regulations of the governments of the countries visited.

10. Cancellation Refund Policy

In the event of cancellation by consumer after confirmation of the booking, the deposit is non-refundable and non-transferable. After payment is made, refunds will be made as follows:

Cancellation	Refund
More than 30 days prior to departure	100% of tour cost
30-11 days prior to departure	90% of tour cost
10-2 days prior to departure	50% of tour cost
Less than two days before departure	No refund

(1) Written notice of cancellation must be received by Travel Service.

(2) In addition to the above stated cancellation charges, if airline tickets have already been issued at the time of cancellation(regardless of a number of days prior to departure), the consumer will be burdened with an additional airline cancellation penalty and service charge pursuant to the airlines rules and regulations.

(3) When a participant cannot complete the tour for any reason, the unused portion of the tour is nonrefundable. No refund will be made to those participants who have failed to secure valid travel documents such as passport or visas.

11. Complaints and Arbitration

(1) If Tourist has any complaints during the tour, Tourist may inform the local guide or the local representative specified by Travel Service. Failure to promptly notify Travel Service of the complaint may reduce or eliminate any compensation that may be payable. In case that a satisfactory remedy is not achieved, Tourist may submit a written complaint to Travel Service within thirty

days from the end of the tour. Complaints received by Travel Service will be dealt with promptly and fairly within the terms of these conditions.

（2）All disputes arising in connection with this contract or any modification or extension thereof, should be settled amicably through negotiations. In case no settlement can be reached, the case in dispute shall then be submitted for arbitration to Beijing Arbitration Commission, China.

12. Validity

This agreement is valid from September 10, 2016 to October 28, 2016 and effective upon signed by the two parties.

13. Original Text

This contract is written in English, in two originals, one for each party.

Travel Service   Tourist

Tong Yang
General Manager   Wayne Carter
BJ ** Travel service
（朱华:《英语导游实务教程》,北京大学出版社,2009 年。）

02 旅行社信函

Date：May 29th, 2016

Dear Sirs，

Would you please proceed with land arrangements in Beijing for the group，according to the itinerary enclosed and what is listed below：

1. Members：   Seventeen paying members and one free tour leader
2. Rooms required：   Eight double rooms and one single room，each with private bath.
3. Hotels：   4-star Grand Hotel or 5-star Grand Hotel
4. Tr./SS：   An air-conditioned coach for transfer and sightseeing
5. Meals：   As given in the itinerary
6. Airport tax：   Not included.

We look forward to receiving your confirmation for the group at your earliest convenience.

Yours Sincerely，

Tong Yang

General Manager

BJ ** Travel Service

（朱华：《英语导游实务教程》，北京大学出版社，2009 年。）

03 旅游行程单

China Discovery Tour

Cities to visit：Beijing, Xi'an, Nanjing, Shanghai

Quotation：US ＄ 2500/P. P.

Arriving： 9：15, August 6th, 2016. Flight CA1＊＊, Beijing Capital International Airport(PEK)

Departure：21：30, August 15th, 2016. Flight CA1＊＊, Shanghai Pudong International Airport(PVG)(Booked by travel agency)

Tour Description：The 10-day tour will present a panoramic view of China, including the modern capital city of Beijing：Tian'anmen Square, the Great Wall and the Forbidden City；the ancient capital city of Xi'an：Terracotta Warriors and Horses；the beautiful city of Nanjing：Dr. Sun Yat-sen's Mausoleum, the Ming Tomb, and the Confucius Temple；Two-day Shopping in Shanghai. It's a tour of Chinese history, a tour of Chinese culture and a tour of Chinese nature.

Day 01(6th August)

Arrive in Beijing, capital of China, by Air China at 9：15 on August 6 morning(Beijing Time), met at the airport and transferred to Beijing Shangri-la Hotel. Welcome dinner in the evening, free at leisure for the rest of the day. (LD)

Day 02(7th August)

The morning tour：Tian'anmen Square and the Forbidden City, have a stroll on the world's largest square in the city center, cross the Golden Water Bridge and visit the well preserved imperial palace complex, the Forbidden City. Back to the hotel after lunch for a short break. At 14：00, visit the National Museum mainly to see cultural relics unearthed in Beijing. Then visit the Temple of Heaven, which was initially built for emperors to worship the god of heaven. Beijing Roast Duck dinner in Quanjude Restaurant in the evening. (BLD)

Day 03(8th August)

In the morning, visit the Badaling Great Wall, one of the most developed and representative sections of the wonderful military projects. For visitors it has long been a wish to ascend the wall and appreciate it winding up and down over the mountain ridges. In the afternoon, the trip will be extended to the Sacred Way and the Ming Tombs with its precious stone palace underground. On the way back to downtown, stop off at the Bird's Nest (Olympic National Stadium) to watch the marvelous building at close quarters. Back to hotel to have dinner at about 18:00. After that, enjoy the national quintessential opera "Beijing Opera" free of charge. (BLD)

Day 04 (9th August)

After breakfast, go to visit the Summer Palace, the largest and best-preserved royal palace famous for its amazing landscape and classical architecture, and Beijing Zoo to see Chinese national treasure, the giant pandas eating bamboos, playing or sleeping in real life. Following the morning activities, proceed to the Lama Temple which used to be the national centre of Lama Administration in Qing Dynasty. The trip draws to an end after a Hutong (lane) tour to get a feel of the old Beijing. Back to hotel about 17:30, have dinner, go to watch Legend of Kungfu Show. Pack luggage before going to bed; enjoy the last night in Beijing. (BLD)

Day 05 (10th August)

Leave luggage out of room at 6:30, finish breakfast and check out of hotel before 7:00. Leave for airport at 7:10, flight to Xi'an at 9:25, and arrive at 11:20. Take the coach to visit the City Wall, and then to Sheraton Xi'an North City Hotel and have lunch there (local specialty of Pita Bread Soaked in Lamb Soup). After lunch, visit the Museum of Qin Shi Huang Terracotta Warriors and Horses, one of the most important archaeological finds in the 20th century, and a local village to see the country of northern China and farmers' life. Back to the hotel around 17:00, take a short break for half an hour and then watch the Muslim Quarter after the Dumpling dinner. Pack luggage before going to bed. (BLD)

Day 06 (11th August)

Take luggage to coach. Start with the visit to the Forest of Steles, then to the

Big Wild Goose Pagoda, which was first built in the Tang Dynasty for the storage of Buddhist scriptures taken from India by Monk Xuanzang. Lunch at airport restaurant. Flight to Nanjing at 16: 10, arrive at 18: 35. Check in Nanjing Jinling Hotel. (BLD)

Day 07(12th August)

Start tour with the visit to Dr. Sun Yat-sen Mausoleum. Dr. Sun Yat-sen, father of Modern China, fought against the imperial Qing government. Then move on to the Ming Tomb, the only world cultural heritage site in Nanjing. Enjoy salty duck and duck blood and starch noodle soup for lunch. After lunch, go to visit Linggu Temple and then Hongshan Forest Zoo with more than 3,000 animals including rare native species like Asian elephant, white tiger, ginger-furred snub-nosed monkeys. (BLD)

Day 08(13th August)

After breakfast, go to the Yangtze River Bridge, the first bridge over the Yangtze River, designed and built independently by China, and then visit Presidential Palace, which is a history book of 600 years' Chinese modern history from the Ming Dynasty to the Qing Dynasty. In the afternoon, sightsee in the Confucius Temple, which has a history of over 1,500 years. The area around it is a busy and lively shopping area, and a place full of restaurants of local food and snack bars, and Qinhuai Scenic Zone. Local snacks for supper. Boating on Qinhuai River in the evening. Pack luggage before going to bed. (BLD)

Day 09(14th August)

G75 ** by CRH(China Railway High-speed) to Shanghai at 7: 20. Enjoy the pleasant day starting with a visit to Shanghai Museum. Have a bird's-eye view of the city from the Oriental Pearl TV Tower, the third tallest TV and radio tower in the world. After that, take a nice walk along the Bund, Shanghai famed waterfront promenade, and Nanjing Road, China No. 1 commercial street for shopping, especially Plaza 66, a commercial and office complex in Shanghai, consisting of a shopping mall and two skyscrapers. With 66 floors, a plaza where you can get close to famous designers and models from all over the world. Finish the day's tour with the Old Town Market. (BLD)

Day 10(15th August)

Take luggage and carry-on to the coach by 8: 00 in the morning. First a visit to Shanghai Financial Center in the new and fast-developing Lujiazui for shopping by Metro Line 2. Shopping at Super Brand Mall, a huge shopping complex with various entertainments and shopping facilities. It has 13 floors and hundreds of shops, including 70 restaurants and cafes. After dinner, go to the airport for CA1 ** departing at 21: 30 back to Australia. (BLD)

04　航空旅行服务备忘录

AIR TOUR CHECKLIST

Before your clients arrive, have you:

☐ Checked with the supervisor about check-in procedures?

☐ Checked with the supervisor about client seat assignments?

☐ Confirmed all special seating and meal requests?

☐ Made sure you, the escort, have a seat?

☐ Determined from which gate your flight will leave?

☐ Figured out where restaurants, restrooms, and shops are?

As your clients arrive, have you:

☐ Asked clients if they brought passports, visas, etc.?

☐ Asked clients if they brought airline tickets(or distributed them)?

☐ Checked off their luggage for future tracking purposes?

☐ Passed out necessary documents?

☐ Informed them of the departure time and gate?

☐ Warned them to protect their valuables?

☐ Made sure everyone has arrived?

Aboard the aircraft, have you:

☐ Introduced yourself to the flight crew?

☐ Collected airline tickets from clients(if company policy)?

☐ Organized baggage-claim stubs?

Upon arrival at your destination, have you:

☐ Sought out the ground operator?

☐ Helped organize clients' luggage claims?

☐ Found a porter to help you?

☐ Made sure all luggage has arrived?

☐ Taken a baggage count before loading the transfer coach?

☐ Taken a head count before leaving on the transfer coach?

05 中国签证申请表

中华人民共和国签证申请表
Visa Application Form of the People's Republic of China
(For the Mainland of China only)

申请人必须如实、完整、清楚地填写本表格。请逐项在空白处用中文或英文大写字母打印填写，或在□内打√选择。如有关项目不适用，请写"无"。The applicant should fill in this form truthfully, completely and clearly. Please type the answer in capital English letters in the space provided or tick (√) the relevant box to select. If some of the items do not apply, please type N/A or None.

一、个人信息　Part 1: Personal Information

1.1 英文姓名 Full English name as in passport	姓 Last name	粘贴一张近期正面免冠、浅色背景的彩色护照照片。 照片/Photo Affix one recent color passport photo (full face, front view, bareheaded and against a plain light colored background).
	中间名 Middle name	
	名 First name	
1.2 中文姓名 Name in Chinese	1.3 别名或曾用名 Other name(s)	
1.4 性别 Sex　□ 男 M　□ 女 F	1.5 出生日期 DOB(yyyy-mm-dd)	
1.6 现有国籍 Current nationality(ies)	1.7 曾有国籍 Former nationality(ies)	
1.8 出生地点(市、省/州、国) Place of birth(city, province/state, country)		
1.9 身份证/公民证号码 Local ID/Citizenship number		
1.10 护照/旅行证件种类 Passport/Travel document type	□ 外交 Diplomatic □ 公务、官员 Service or Official □ 普通 Ordinary □ 其他证件(请说明) Other(Please specify):	
1.11 护照号码 Passport number	1.12 签发日期 Date of issue(yyyy-mm-dd)	
1.13 签发地点 Place of issue	1.14 失效日期 Date of expiry(yyyy-mm-dd)	

1.15 当前职业 （可选多项） Current occupation(s)	☐ 商人 Businessperson ☐ 公司职员 　Company employee ☐ 演艺人员 Entertainer ☐ 工人/农民 Industrial/ 　Agricultural worker ☐ 学生 Student ☐ 乘务人员 Crew member ☐ 自雇 Self-employed ☐ 无业 Unemployed ☐ 退休 Retired ☐ 其他（请说明）Other(Please specify)：	☐ 前/现任议员 Former/incumbent 　member of parliament 　职位 Position ＿＿＿＿＿＿＿ ☐ 前/现任政府官员 Former/ 　incumbent government official 　职位 Position ＿＿＿＿＿＿＿ ☐ 军人 Military personnel 　职位 Position ＿＿＿＿＿＿＿ ☐ 非政府组织人员 NGO staff ☐ 宗教人士 Religious personnel ☐ 新闻从业人员 Staff of media
1.16 受教育程度 Education	☐ 研究生 Postgraduate ☐ 其他（请说明）Other(Please specify)：	☐ 大学 College

1.17 工作单位/ 学校 Employer/School	名称 Name	联系电话 Phone number
	地址 Address	邮政编码 Zip Code

1.18 家庭住址 Home address		1.19 邮政编码 Zip Code
1.20 电话/手机 Home/mobile phone number		1.21 电子邮箱 E-mail address

1.22 婚姻状况
Marital status　☐ 已婚 Married　☐ 单身 Single
　　　　　　　☐ 其他 Other(Please specify)：

1.23 主要家庭成 员（配偶、子女、 父母等，可另纸） Major family members(spouse, children, parents, etc., may type on separate paper)	姓名 Name	国籍 Nationality	职业 Occupation	关系 Relationship

1.24 紧急联络人信息 Emergency Contact	姓名 Name	手机 Mobile phone number
	与申请人的关系 Relationship with the applicant	

1.25 申请人申请签证时所在的国家或地区 Country or territory where the applicant is located when applying for this visa	

二、旅行信息　Part 2：Travel Information

2.1 申请 入境事由 Major purpose of your visit	☐ 官方访问 Official Visit ☐ 旅游 Tourism ☐ 交流、考察、访问 　Non-business visit ☐ 商业贸易 Business & Trade ☐ 人才引进 As introduced talent ☐ 执行乘务 As crew member ☐ 过境 Transit	☐ 常驻外交、领事、国际组织人员 　As resident diplomat, consul or 　staff of international organization ☐ 永久居留 As permanent resident ☐ 工作 Work ☐ 寄养 As child in foster care
	☐ 短期探望中国公民或者具有中国永久居留资格的外国人 Short-term visit to Chinese citizen or foreigner with Chinese permanent residence status	☐ 与中国公民或者具有中国永久居留资格的外国人家庭团聚居留超过 180 日 Family reunion for over 180 days with Chinese citizen or foreigner with Chinese permanent residence status
	☐ 短期探望因工作、学习等事由在中国停留居留的外国人 Short-term visit to foreigner residing in China due to work, study or other reasons	☐ 长期探望因工作、学习等事由在中国居留的外国人 As accompanying family member of foreigner residing in China due to work, study or other reasons
	☐ 短期学习 Short-term study for less than 180 days	☐ 长期学习 Long-term study for over 180 days
	☐ 短期采访报道 As journalist for temporary news coverage	☐ 外国常驻中国新闻机构记者 As resident journalist
	☐ 其他(请说明)Other (Please specify)：	
2.2 计划 入境次数 Intended number of entries	☐ 一次(自签发之日起 3 个月有效) One entry valid for 3 months from the date of issue ☐ 二次(自签发之日起 3 - 6 个月有效) Two entries valid for 3 to 6 months from the date of issue ☐ 半年多次(自签发之日起 6 个月有效) Multiple entries valid for 6 months from the date of issue ☐ 一年多次(自签发之日起 1 年有效) Multiple entries valid for 1 year from the date of issue ☐ 其他(请说明)Other (Please specify)：	
2.3 是否申请加急服务 Are you applying for express service? 注:加急服务须经领事官员批准,将加收费用。 Note：Express service needs approval of consular officials, and extra fees may apply.	☐ 是 Yes　　☐ 否 No	

续表

2.4 本次行程预计首次抵达中国的日期 Expected date of your first entry into China on this trip （yyyy-mm-dd）		
2.5 预计行程中单次在华停留的最长天数 Longest intended stay in China among all entries		Days
2.6 在中国境内 行程（按时间顺 序，可附另纸 填写） Itinerary in China （in time sequence, may type on separate paper）	日期 Date	详细地址 Detailed address
2.7 谁将承担在中国期间的费用? Who will pay for your travel and expenses during your stay in China?		
2.8 中国境内 邀请单位或 个人信息 Information of inviter in China	姓名或名称 Name	
	地址 Address	
	联系电话 Phone number	
	与申请人关系 Relationship with the applicant	
2.9 是否曾经获得过中国签证? 如有，请说明最近 一次获得中国签证的时间和地点。Have you ever been granted a Chinese visa? If applicable, please specify the date and place of the last time you were granted the visa.		
2.10 过去 12 个月中访问的其他国家或地区 Other countries or territories you visited in the last 12 months		

三、其他事项　Part 3: Other Information

3.1 是否曾在中国超过签证或居留许可允许的期限停留? Have you ever overstayed your visa or residence permit in China?	□是 Yes　□否 No
3.2 是否曾经被拒绝签发中国签证，或被拒绝进入中国? Have you ever been refused a visa for China, or been refused entry into China?	□是 Yes　□否 No

续表

3.3 是否在中国或其他国家有犯罪记录？Do you have any criminal record in China or any other country?	□是 Yes　□否 No
3.4 是否具有以下任一种情形 Are you experiencing any of the following conditions? ① 严重精神障碍 Serious mental disorder ② 传染性肺结核病 Infectious pulmonary tuberculosis ③ 可能危害公共卫生的其他传染病 Other infectious disease of public health hazards	□是 Yes　□否 No
3.5 近30日内是否前往过流行性疾病传染的国家或地区？Did you visit countries or territories affected by infectious diseases in the last 30 days?	□是 Yes　□否 No

3.6 如果对3.1到3.5的任何一个问题选择"是"，请在下面详细说明。
If you select Yes to any questions from 3.1 to 3.5, please give details below.

3.7 如果有本表未涉及而需专门陈述的其他与签证申请相关的事项，请在此或另纸说明。If you have more information about your visa application other than the above to declare, please give details below or type on a separate paper.

3.8 如申请人护照中的偕行人与申请人一同旅行，请将偕行人照片粘贴在下面并填写偕行人信息。If someone else travels and shares the same passport with the applicant, please affix their photos and give their information below.

偕行人信息 Information	偕行人1 Person 1 粘贴照片于此 Affix Photo here	偕行人2 Person 2 粘贴照片于此 Affix Photo here	偕行人3 Person 3 粘贴照片于此 Affix Photo here
姓名 Full name			
性别 Sex			
生日 DOB(yyyy-mm-dd)			

四、声明及签名　Part 4：Declaration & Signature

4.1 我声明,我已阅读并理解此表所有内容要求,并愿就所填报信息和申请材料的真实性承担一切法律后果。

I hereby declare that I have read and understood all the questions in this application and shall bear all the legal consequences for the authenticity of the information and materials I provided.

4.2 我理解,能否获得签证、获得何种签证、入境次数以及有效期、停留期等将由领事官员决定,任何不实、误导或填写不完整均可能导致签证申请被拒绝或被拒绝进入中国。

I understand that whether to issue a visa, type of visa, number of entries, validity and duration of each stay will be determined by consular official, and that any false, misleading or incomplete statement may result in the refusal of a visa for or denial of entry into China.

4.3 我理解,根据中国法律,申请人即使持有中国签证仍有可能被拒绝入境。

I understand that, according to Chinese law, applicant may be refused entry into China even if a visa is granted.

➡申请人签名　　　　　　　　　　　　　　日期

Applicant's signature：_____　Date（yyyy-mm-dd）：_____

注：未满 18 周岁的未成年人须由父母或监护人代签。

Note：The parent or guardian shall sign on behalf of a minor under 18 years of age.

五、他人代填申请表时填写以下内容　Part 5：If the application form is completed by another person on the applicant's behalf, please fill out the information of the one who completes the form

5.1 姓名 Name		5.2 与申请人关系 Relationship with the applicant	
5.3 地址 Address		5.4 电话 Phone number	

5.5 声明 Declaration

我声明本人是根据申请人要求而协助填表,证明申请人理解并确认表中所填写内容准确无误。

I declare that I have assisted in the completion of this form at the request of the applicant and that the applicant understands and agrees that the information provided is true and correct.

代填人签名/Signature：_____　　　　日期/Date（yyyy-mm-dd）：_____

06 外国人出入境卡

外国人出境卡 DEPARTURE CARD
请交边防检查员查验 For Immigration clearance

姓 Family name

名 Given names

护照号码 Passport No.

出生日期 Date of birth　年Year　月Month　日Day

国籍 Nationality

航班号/船名/车次 Flight No./Ship's name/Train No.

男 Male □　女 Female □

以上申明真实准确。
I hereby declare that the statement given above is true and accurate.

签名 Signature

妥善保留此卡，如遗失将会对出境造成不便。
Retain this card in your possession, failure to do so may delay your departure from China.

请注意背面重要提示。See the back →

外国人入境卡 ARRIVAL CARD
请交边防检查员查验 For Immigration clearance

姓 Family name

名 Given names

护照号码 Passport No.

国籍 Nationality

在华住址 Intended Address in China

出生日期 Date of birth　年Year　月Month　日Day

签证号码 Visa No.

签证签发地 Place of Visa Issuance

航班号/船名/车次 Flight No./Ship's name/Train No.

男 Male □　女 Female □

入境事由（只能填写一项）Purpose of visit (one only)

会议/商务 Conference/Business □　访问 Visit □　学习 Study □

探亲访友 Visiting friends or relatives □　就业 Employment □　观光/休闲 Sightseeing in leisure □

返回常住地 Return home □　定居 Settle down □　其他 other □

以上申明真实准确。
I hereby declare that the statement given above is true and accurate.

签名 Signature

Important Notice

1. Aliens who do not lodge at hotels, guesthouses or inns shall, within 24 hours (72 hours in rural areas) of entry, go through accommodation registration at local police station.

2. Aliens holding visas Z, X or J-1 shall, within 30 days of entry, apply for Residence Permits to the exit-entry department of the public security bureau of the city where the applicants reside.

3. Aliens shall not be employed in China without permission of the competent authorities of the Chinese Government.

4. Aliens who reside or stay in China shall carry with themselves their passports or Residence Permits for possible examination.

5. In case of emergency, please dial 110 to seek help from police.

07 中国海关进出境旅客行李物品申报单

<table>
<tr><td colspan="2">

中华人民共和国海关
进出境旅客行李物品申报单

请仔细阅读申报单背面的填单须知后填报

姓　名 □□□　名 □□□　男 □ 女 □

出生日期 □□□□ 年 □□ 月 □□ 日 国籍（地区）□□□

护照（进出境证件）号码 □□□□□□□□□□□□

进境旅客填写	出境旅客填写
来自何地 □□□	前往何地 □□□
进境航班号/车次/船名 □□□	出境航班号/车次/船名 □□□
进境日期：□□ 年 □□ 月 □□ 日	出境日期：□□ 年 □□ 月 □□ 日
携带有下列物品请在"□"划√	携带有下列物品请在"□"划√
□ 1. 动植物及其产品、微生物、生物制品、人体组织、血液及其制品	□ 1. 文物、濒危动植物及其制品、生物物种资源、金银等贵重金属
□ 2. 居民旅客在境外获取总值超过人民币5,000元的物品	□ 2. 居民旅客携带需复带进境的单价超过人民币5,000元的照相机、摄像机、手提电脑等旅行自用物品
□ 3. 非居民旅客拟留在境内总值超过人民币2,000元的物品	
□ 4. 超过1,500毫升的酒精饮料（酒精含量12°以上），或超过400支香烟，或超过100支雪茄，或超过500克烟丝	□ 3. 超过20,000元人民币现钞，或超过折合美元5,000元外币现钞
□ 5. 超过20,000元人民币现钞，或超过折合美元5,000元外币现钞	□ 4. 货物、货样、广告品
□ 6. 分离运输行李、货物、货样、广告品	□ 5. 其它需要向海关申报的物品
□ 7. 其它需要向海关申报的物品	

携带有上述物品的，请详细填写如下清单

品名/币种	型　号	数　量	金　额	海关批注

我已经阅读本申报单背面所列事项，并保证所有申报属实。

旅客签名 □□□

</td><td>

一、重要提示：

1. 没有携带应向海关申报物品的旅客，无需填写本申报单，可选择"无申报通道"（又称"绿色通道"，标识为"●"）通关。

2. 携带有应向海关申报物品的旅客，应当填写本申报单，向海关书面申报，并选择"申报通道"（又称"红色通道"，标识为"■"）通关。海关免于监管的人员以及随同成人旅行的16周岁以下旅客可不填写申报单。

3. 请妥善保管本申报单，以便在返程时继续使用。

4. 本申报单所称"居民旅客"系指其通常定居地在中国关境内的旅客，"非居民旅客"系指其通常定居地在中国关境外的旅客。

5. 不如实申报的旅客将承担相应法律责任。

二、中华人民共和国禁止进境物品：

1. 各种武器、仿真武器、弹药及爆炸物品；

2. 伪造的货币及伪造的有价证券；

3. 对中国政治、经济、文化、道德有害的印刷品、胶卷、照片、唱片、影片、录音带、录像带、激光唱盘、激光视盘、计算机存储介质及其它物品；

4. 各种烈性毒药；

5. 鸦片、吗啡、海洛因、大麻以及其它能使人成瘾的麻醉品、精神药物；

6. 新鲜水果、茄科蔬菜、活动物(犬、猫除外)、动物产品、动植物病原体和害虫及其它有害生物、动物尸体、土壤、转基因生物材料、动植物疫情流行的国家和地区的有关动植物及其产品和其它应检物；

7. 有碍人畜健康的、来自疫区的以及其它能传播疾病的食品、药品或其它物品。

三、中华人民共和国禁止出境物品

1. 列入禁止进境范围的所有物品；

2. 内容涉及国家秘密的手稿、印刷品、胶卷、照片、唱片、影片、录音带、录像带、激光唱盘、激光视盘、计算机存储介质及其它物品；

3. 珍贵文物及其它禁止出境的文物；

4. 濒危的和珍贵的动植物(均含标本)及其种子和繁殖材料。

</td></tr>
</table>

08　旅客健康申报表

PASSENGER'S HEALTH DECLARATION

Name in full _____ Sex _____ Age _____

Nationality _____ Occupation _____

Date of entry _____ Flight No. _____

1. Date & place of departure _____

2. Please mark "√" before the symptom if any now.

   ☐Fever　　☐Rash　　☐Cough　　☐Sore throat　　Bleeding

   ☐Vomiting　☐Diarrhea　☐Jaundice　☐Lymph-gland Swelling

3. Any illness now：Psychosis，Leprosy，AIDS（Inc. AIDS virus carrier），venereal diseases，active pulmonary tuberculosis and other diseases

4. Please mark "√" in the items of the following articles, if you bring any of them with yourself.

   Biologicals _____ Blood products _____ Second-hand clothes _____

5. Name of travel group _____

6. Contact address and host organization in China _____

附中文版

旅客健康申报表

姓名_____性别_____年龄_____

国籍_____职业_____

入境日期_____乘机航班号_____

1. 这次旅行来自何地及出发日期_____

2. 如有以下症状，请在症状前划"√"：

   ☐发烧　　☐皮疹　　☐咳嗽　　☐咽喉痛　　☐出血

   ☐呕吐　　☐腹泻　　☐黄疸　　☐淋巴结肿

3. 现在是否患有：精神病、麻风病、艾滋病（包括艾滋病毒带毒者）、性病、开放性肺结核和其他疾病？

4. 如随身携带下列物品，请在下列项目内划"√"：

   生物制品_____血制品_____旧衣服_____

5. 旅游团名称_____

6. 在华住址和接待单位_____

09　游客调查表

CLIENT SURVEY

Dear Client: Could you take a few moments to complete this survey? Your comments will help us to evaluate this tour and determine which changes might be worth considering. Thanks for your input. And we sincerely hope that you had a wonderful tour vacation.

TOUR: _____　DEPARTURE DATE: _____

TOUR ESCORT'S NAME: _____

Item(if applicable)	Excellent	Very Good	Good	Poor	Comment
Attractions visited	☐	☐	☐	☐	_____
Driver's　courtesy	☐	☐	☐	☐	_____
Driver's　skill	☐	☐	☐	☐	_____
Escort's　courtesy	☐	☐	☐	☐	_____
Escort's　knowledge	☐	☐	☐	☐	_____
Escort's　personality	☐	☐	☐	☐	_____
Escort's speaking ability	☐	☐	☐	☐	_____
Flights	☐	☐	☐	☐	_____
Hotels	☐	☐	☐	☐	_____
Motor coach condition	☐	☐	☐	☐	_____
Motor coach ride	☐	☐	☐	☐	_____
Restaurants	☐	☐	☐	☐	_____
Ship	☐	☐	☐	☐	_____
Shopping time	☐	☐	☐	☐	_____
Sightseeing	☐	☐	☐	☐	_____
Train	☐	☐	☐	☐	_____
Other _____	☐	☐	☐	☐	_____

Please fill out the following. It will be kept confidential.

Your age _____　　Your sex _____　　Your yearly income $ _____

Yearly expense on vacation travel(one person) $ _____

Your profession _____

The most you can imagine yourself paying for a tour package $ _____

Married☐　Single☐　Divorced☐　Widowed☐

In your opinion, what is the ideal number of days a tour should have? _____

Where will you probably go on the next tour you take? _____

Copyright @ Delmar Publishers

10 旅游征求意见表

Tour Questionaire

Thank you for taking time to complete this card Date _____ Time _____ A. M/P. M How many in your party? _____ Server's Name _____		
HOSPITALITY		
Were you greeted as you entered?	☐YES	☐NO
Did the hostess/host seat you?	☐YES	☐NO
Did server introduce her/himself by name?	☐YES	☐NO
Did server say goodbye and invite you to come again?	☐YES	☐NO
FOOD AND SERVICE		
Was food served promptly?	☐YES	☐NO
Was your order correct?	☐YES	☐NO
Was food properly prepared?	☐YES	☐NO
Did you receive smiling service?	☐YES	☐NO
ENVIRONMENT		
Did our staff have a neat, clean appearance?	☐YES	☐NO
Were your dining area and dining utensils clean?	☐YES	☐NO
Was the restaurant clean overall?	☐YES	☐NO

附中文版

旅游征求意见表

谢谢您填写此表 日期_____时间_____ 你们一行几人? _____ 服务员姓名_____		
接待		
您进来时是否有被问好?	☐是	☐否
服务员是否请您入座?	☐是	☐否
服务员是否做自我介绍?	☐是	☐否
服务员是否向您道别,并欢迎您的再次光临?	☐是	☐否
食品及服务		
上菜速度快吗?	☐是	☐否
上的菜对吗?	☐是	☐否
食物合胃口吗?	☐是	☐否
您受到友好礼貌的服务吗?	☐是	☐否
环境		
本店工作人员仪表整洁吗?	☐是	☐否
用餐区域及餐具清洁吗?	☐是	☐否
总体来说餐厅清洁吗?	☐是	☐否

（朱华:《英语导游实务教程》,北京大学出版社,2009 年。）

11 物品损失报告

DAMAGED PROPERTY REPORT

ESCORT FILLING OUT THIS FORM：_____

CLIENT'S NAME：_____

CLIENT'S ADDRESS：_____

CLIENT'S PHONE NUMBER：(_____)_____

TOUR AND DEPARTURE DATE：_____

Describe item damaged：

_____

_____

Describe nature of damage：

_____

_____

Describe circumstances that caused damage：

_____

_____

Describe how and when you first discovered the damage：

_____

_____

Answer the following：

Did you, on the first day of the tour, notice that item was NOT worn or damaged?

☐Yes ☐No

Did you, on the first day of the tour, notice that the item WAS worn or damage?

☐Yes ☐No

If so, did you notify the client? ☐Yes ☐No

Did you ask the client if he or she had insurance that might cover the damage?

☐Yes ☐No

Nature of insurance：☐Homeowner's ☐Traveler's ☐Credit Card ☐Other

Name of insuring company：_____

Other comments：_____

_____

Copyright @ Delmar Publishers

12　感谢信

June 20, 2016

Dear Mr. Tong,

Thank you so much for providing what we believe to be the world's most high-quality cultural and culinary tour. The scenic spots, accommodation, shows and food you arranged during our tour in China were amazing. We were also impressed by the friendliness of the Chinese people. You all made us feel so welcome. It was truly a most enjoyable experience.

The service for our 10 day tour of China was very well done by your travel service. We had good guides and drivers. Our guides are very knowledgeable about the cities and the scenic spots, and we have learned a great deal from them. We really appreciated the cold water they prepared during our tour. Our guides were very flexible and when we wanted to change our itinerary or cancel one of our sightseeing destinations they were very understanding and gave us wonderful suggestions. We can't give too much compliment for our guides' work!

Our guide in Beijing was absolutely delightful and so much fun to be with. His memory in historical knowledge is amazing. We hope that one day Jiang Min would come to visit our family in Australia and stay at our home. We have sons the same age as Jiang Min, too. All your drivers were absolutely professional in every way, and Mr. Zhang, our driver in Beijing, has earned a more special place in our hearts. Nothing was ever any trouble to him and we felt that we were in safety all the time. We hope you will pass our special kind wishes to him on our behalf.

We had our meals at wonderful restaurants. We like Chinese food and have learned a lot about Chinese food culture. We were lucky to have had many chances to know about and buy Chinese local produce and products. The things are really wonderful and cheap. We were able to bring back many nice and special things from the tour for our families and friends.

We really enjoyed our tour in China. Thank you, thank the Travel Service and thank all the guides. We certainly would travel with your travel service when we are in China next time.

Yours sincerely,

Wayne Carter

（朱华:《英语导游实务教程》,北京大学出版社,2009 年。）

13 投诉信

July 12, 2016

BJ ** Travel Service
*** , Block, Zhongshan Road,
Beijing

Attn: Mr. Tong Yang
Dear Mr. Tong,

We made a 10-day trip in China arranged by your travel service last month. We had a good time for most of the time. However, we were dissatisfied with something unhappy which happened during our travel.

First, when we were in Beijing, the local guide took us to various souvenir and curio stores in the two-day tour. It is true that we did want to buy some souvenirs to bring home; however, shopping for one or two times was enough because we came here for sightseeing after all. With too much time spent on shopping, our tour in scenic spots was always in a hurry. It occurred often that we had hardly visited half of a tourist site when we were asked to leave.

Second, according to the contract concluded between us, we were to stay in a five-star hotel. However, we were transferred to a three-star hotel where air conditioners broke down during our stay. The heat of June in Beijing was nothing for the citizen there, but so unbearable for us that we couldn't fall asleep at night.

Therefore, we request you to give us an explanation and compensate us for 300 dollars per person due to your poor arrangement.

We are looking forward to your prompt reply.

Sincerely yours,

Ted Hunter

（朱华：《英语导游实务教程》，北京大学出版社，2009 年。）

参考文献
References

［1］朱歧新:《北京名胜游览》,中国旅游出版社,2008 年。

［2］陈准民:《实用经贸英语口语》(修订版),对外经济贸易大学出版社,2008 年。

［3］凌丽琴,邱小樱:《导游技能实训教程》,江苏大学出版社,2013 年。

［4］易玉婷,汪峰:《英语导游实务——导游业务部分》,国防工业出版社,2012 年。

［5］朱华:《旅游英语教程》,高等教育出版社,2011 年。

［6］比尔鲍:《朗文现代酒店业英语》,外语教学与研究出版社,2005 年。

［7］滕悦然:《酒店餐饮企业管理工具箱:酒店前台常用英语口语大全》,化学工业出版社,2014 年。

［8］赵晓芳:《星级酒店常用英语》,广东经济出版社,2012 年。

［9］杨静怡:《新职业英语:酒店英语》,外语教学与研究出版社,2010 年。

［10］陈丽芳:《酒店英语口语》,北京师范大学出版社,2012 年。

［11］杨静怡:《旅游与酒店专业实用英语》,中国劳动社会保障出版社,2015 年。

［12］云丽虹:《实用酒店英语》,上海交通大学出版社,2015 年。

［13］胡扬政:《现代酒店服务英语》,清华大学出版社,2013 年。

［14］许红,张婷:《旅游英语》,中国林业出版社,2009 年。

［15］李仕敏,翁莉:《导游英语》,中国铁道出版社,2013 年。

［16］国家旅游局:《走遍中国:中国优秀导游词精选(英文版)》,王军,等译,中国旅游出版社,2000 年。

［17］江苏省旅游局:《走遍江苏(英文版)》,中国林业出版社,2002 年。

［18］赵宏:《全新实用中英文导游词范文》,西安交通大学出版社,2014 年。

［19］Marc Mancini. *Conducting Tours*. Delmar Thomson Learning, 2000.

［20］http://news. xinhuanet. com/english/special/2012 – 10/11/c_131899933. htm.

［21］ http://wenku. baidu. com/link? url = _vqOw61t5xHj7396MjyOFu2TsOyGz-
b6uEg8IE-ZQKpDrLiWNgSq34vHNQkXe4F2nBTkk6CMXGHJa3sp_n2vAJo-
IQBdMzhbtd7uw9WO7R-Ei.

［22］ http://www. chinatours. com/travel-guide/yangtze-river-cruise/attractions/
xiaoling-mausoleum-of-ming-dynasty. html.